SHADOWS

IN THE

DARKNESS

Can you run from
something you cannot see?

M.E. FERREIRA

SHADOWS

IN THE

DARKNESS

M.E. FERREIRA

In memory of my loving parents

ACKNOWLEDGEMENTS

For all of our hilarious conversations and good times.
– *My editor*

For motivating me daily through my long hours of writing.
– *My son and daughter-in-law*

For helping to jog my memory and reminisce
on past times. – *Elaine and Maureen*

For listening to my story and telling me the
world needed to hear it. – *Dr. Johnson*

CONTENTS

PROLOGUE

A picture-perfect bride. The exquisite white satin gown enhances her slim silhouette whilst embracing her curves. The diamond headpiece twinkles atop her glossy black hair and her flawless make-up accentuates her twin dimples, velvet brown eyes and plump lips.

It's the happiest day of her life, isn't it? She certainly looks the part. No one will see the cold dread trembling through her, no one will spot what's underneath the artful make-up. The bruises, both inside and out, are well hidden. As she knows only too well, appearances can be deceptive…

1

ENTER STAGE RIGHT

I am draped in a white tablecloth and have my best white cardigan over my head.

"Don't forget to look amazed," I instruct my sister Kimberly through the closed bedroom door.

"Okay," comes her sleepy reply.

I make my grand entrance as the beautiful bride, Princess Peony. Instead of looking amazed, Kimberly is lying on her bed, yawning.

"Get up!" I hiss. "You are supposed to be waiting for me at the altar."

"Do I have to be Prince Charming again?" moans Kimberly.

She knows the answer to that: I am always the princess or the queen, so my little sister has to play all the other parts as well as playing the audience. I may be only seven years old, but I know that I am destined to be an actress. I love creating little dramas for us to act out in our bedroom. Whether it's Princess Peony marrying her handsome true love, or Queen Amelia ruling her kingdom with fierce wisdom, I am always the leading lady – as well as the writer, director and make-up artist. Sometimes, I am a pop star and treat Kimberly to an exclusive concert. Cardigan once again on head (this time it's my long, flowing hair), I sing into my hairbrush and expect my sister to clap thunderously after each number. And woe betide her if she doesn't. Kimberly is two years younger than me and she is usually pretty enthusiastic about these early morning performances. Rarely complaining when I rouse her from her slumbers, she usually goes along with whatever I've dreamed up – unless she's hungry.

"Can't we go down for breakfast?" asks Kimberly.

"Good idea," I reply, throwing off my cardigan veil. Prince Charming can wait. I love food much more than him.

Mealtimes in our house were always merry occasions. We all sat down to eat together, my mum and dad, me and my three younger siblings, Kimberly, brother Jaden, who's five years younger than me and Zoe, the baby of the family. My mum Florence was the most marvellous cook. Like my dad, she was from Jamaica and her food was full of the sunshine and flavours of her Caribbean home. Her food was so prized that she didn't just cook for us, she would also cater for other people's parties and social events. How often the kitchen would be filled with the mouth-watering aroma of spicy curries, fried fish and fragrant rice dishes. I loved her soup best of all. As much as I loved Jamaican food, I also loved British food. Yes, really! This was the reason I looked forward to going to school. Jelly and blancmange were my favourites, along with toad in the hole, meat pies and gravy. I just couldn't get enough of it and would often go up and ask for seconds, much to the surprise of, well, everyone else who was eating the same school dinners as me. I once played Oliver Twist in a school production and had the famous line, "Please sir, can I have some more?" Given how much I loved my food, my mum thought this was the funniest thing and teased me forever about it.

We lived in a quiet corner of north-west London. Our mid-terrace house had a white door with colourful hanging baskets either side and it was the prettiest house on the street. Home was a safe, happy place and that was all to do with our parents. They were our twin towers of strength, each in a very different way. My mum was a force to be reckoned with. You would not argue with Florence, nor would you want to. If Mum told you to be home by 6pm, 'or else', we knew fine well what the 'or else' would be. Like many children in those days, we would go out for the whole day, just so long as we were back by curfew. And like many children at that time, we would get belted if we weren't.

"It's two minutes past!" "Hurry up, run faster." "There she is!"

"Oh no…"

Many's the time the clock had just ticked past 6pm as we raced up the garden path to see Mum standing at the door, belt in hand. Luckily, I was the fastest runner, so was able to dodge past her without being hit, unlike my slower sister Kimberly.

It wasn't that Mum was hard, she just wanted the best for us. She wanted to instil in us discipline and perseverance that would serve us well all our lives. So, she would never accept any excuses.

"Mum, can I go out to play?" "Have you done your chores?" "Most of them…"

"So, is that yes or no?"

By the time Mum fixed you with her stern eye, you knew you were beaten. From a very young age, she taught me how to cook, how to clean and look after the house. I wasn't interested in learning domestic skills because I was going to be a performer, but I did them anyway (not that I had a choice) and I'm glad I did. Mum loved us like a lioness and her tough, practical love was balanced by Dad's softer influence.

When Dad was at home there would be whippy ice cream – with a flake, if we were really lucky. "Who wants a cornet?" he would ask, when the van arrived. And he would never buy an ice-cream just for us. If he had the money, he would buy for all the children out in the street; no one would be left out. And if he didn't have enough money to buy for all of us, he wouldn't buy for anyone at all. That was my kindly dad.

Though he wasn't cash-rich, my dad was ambitious and very proud. He was very good looking and always well turned out in his suit and trilby hat. No one would ever know that this was his one and only suit, which he would wash overnight. He would fill his pockets with lots of coins and put paper in his wallet to make it look as though he had a lot of cash, but he never really did. A jack of all trades, he could turn his hand to many things, from building to carpentry and roofing. He worked hard to bring in the money for his family and whatever cash he had was spent on us. While he only had the one suit, we were always beautifully turned out. If we were happy, he was happy. Dad hated to see us upset, so if he ever told us off, he'd come and make up with us within five minutes. And if he was around when we were late getting back for dinner, he'd sometimes be able to distract Mum until we could slip in unnoticed.

I inherited my ambition from my dad, who would push us hard at school to do well. In between eating school dinners, I worked hard and did well academically. But what I enjoyed most was the performing arts. Dad would come to see all of my performances in school plays and productions I was involved with outside of school. Some of my fellow performers would be almost sick with nerves beforehand, but I loved that feeling of electricity coursing through me before curtain-up. I loved to dance, too. All those feelings and emotions that were bubbling up inside me, I found I could express through movement. I once did so well in a competition that I appeared on the TV, performing on 'Nationwide', which was an early incarnation of 'The One Show'. I thought my dad might explode with pride.

Then came the day when I feared my parents might explode with anger. I walked home, rehearsing what I was going to say to them.

"Something bad happened in school today, but it wasn't my fault…" *No, don't say it was bad.* "There was a bit of trouble today but I didn't start it." *Face it, Amelia, it is never going to sound good, no matter how you say it.* But I also knew I hadn't really done anything wrong. As I approached the house I felt a bit sick. How was I going to tell them?

"I was expelled from school," I blurted out straight away.

"What?" cried my mum.

There was a storm gathering on her face, but before she could say another word, Dad said, "Tell us what happened."

And then it all came tumbling out. I'd had a fight with Joy, a sixth former who lived a few doors down from us. I was not a fighter: even when the so-called 'hard' girls at school used to push and slap me, hoping to get some sort of rise out of me, I just stood there and took it. It was only when they picked on my younger sister Kimberly that I would retaliate. I would fight hard to protect my sister.

But I was Joy's target. For weeks, she had been picking on me, needling me, taunting me, because she thought we were poor. There were some people in our school who, unlike me, were genuinely poor: kids who only got a proper meal at school, or who wore shoes a size too small because they couldn't afford new ones. Their lives were hard enough; I couldn't understand why it would give someone pleasure to ridicule them. So far, I had managed to ignore Joy's taunts; I wasn't going to waste my breath and energy on a bully like her.

"I never said anything back to her, she's just not worth it," I explained to my parents.

"But today I'd just had enough. She started on me in the canteen, throwing bits of bread at me and telling me to eat it because it was free food."

Not only was she insulting me, but she was also insulting my whole family and everything my parents had achieved through their hard work and love. I didn't bother pointing

7

out to Joy that we were one of the few families on the street to own their own house. Sometimes actions spoke louder than words.

"She carried on calling me names in front of everyone when we got out of the canteen, so I just let her have it."

I didn't know where I had got the strength from – maybe from all those weeks of holding my temper – but I was like an unstoppable tornado. After our fight, I knew Joy wouldn't be bothering me again. I wasn't proud of myself – well, maybe a little bit proud, until I understood the consequences of what I'd done. But surely Mum and Dad could see that I had right on my side? If my parents had given us a very strong code of right and wrong, they had also taught us how to stand up for ourselves.

There was a small silence after I had finished speaking. "Did you beat her well?" asked Mum, finally.

"Yes, Mum."

"That's because I fed you well." That was her way of saying, "That's my girl."

My dad's eyes were shining, I couldn't tell if it was with anger or pride. He squeezed my shoulder, put on his jacket and said, "I'm going down to the school, this isn't fair."

But although he pleaded and argued my case, the headteacher stood firm. I was a fifth former and had beaten up a sixth former, who had almost the same status as teachers in our school. There could be no going back for me after that.

I carried on my education at college. And after getting my O and A levels, I started studying dramatic art and film directing. I loved the course and was just about to take my exams when, one spring afternoon, the bottom dropped out of my world.

There was something wrong, I could feel it. I had arrived home from college to find no one there. Instead of a warm, busy kitchen, filled with smells of cooking and laughter, there was an eerie silence. A chill wrapped itself around my heart, squeezing the breath out of me. My dad had a problem with his heart and was in the hospital, waiting to have an operation. But something must have happened because my mum never normally visited him at this time. And where was everyone else? There was no note, no explanation.

I ran out into the street, taking nothing with me, and I hailed the first taxi I saw.

A pair of concerned blue eyes looked through the driver's mirror as I climbed into the back of the cab, tears streaming down my face.

"What's the matter, love?" asked the cabbie.

"I think my dad is dead. Please can you take me to the hospital."

The journey seemed to take forever and there was a heavy weight pressing on my chest, stopping me from breathing.

"Can you hurry please," I implored the driver, needlessly, for he had sensed my urgency and was already doing his best to weave in and out of the London traffic.

I was too late. By the time I got there, Dad had passed. He had died on the operating table during the procedure. He was 47 years old.

I could still picture the reassuring wink he had given me just before he had left home for the hospital. "Don't worry, I'll be good as new once I come home," he'd said. How could there be a home without my dad in it? How could the earth still be turning?

It was two days before my 17th birthday.

2

FAST TRAIN TO ADULTHOOD

The smell of freshly dug earth fills my nostrils. I feel the smooth, warm wood beneath my cheek as I clench my eyes tight shut. *If I lie here long enough, it won't be true.* I can hear someone calling my name, but they sound very far away. *Just let me lie here.* The pounding thud of my heart shudders through my whole body. I don't know what to do: I can't think, I can't breathe, I can't move. I can't do anything but lie here with my dad. *I'm not leaving him.* Eventually, gentle hands prise my fingers free and lead me away from the coffin. As it is lowered into the ground, I can feel a wail of despair welling up from deep within me, but I swallow it down. *Don't cry, girl, don't you cry.* Up above, the sun is shining out of an impossibly blue sky, but it feels to me as if the world has gone dark…

Just before he died, Dad had bought me a coat he knew I

wanted for my birthday. It was brown with a fur collar and it was quality. I wore it on the day of his funeral, and I was glad of it because I couldn't stop shivering, even though it wasn't particularly cold that morning.

It was a terrible day. My heart felt as though it had broken in two and it was so awful to see the pain etched on the faces of my family. Kimberly, Jaden and Zoe looked lost and bewildered, while my mother bore her enormous loss with quiet dignity, only her eyes giving away the desolation she must have been feeling. I don't remember anything about the church service, but once we got to the graveside and I saw the coffin, ready to be lowered into the prepared grave, I threw myself on top of it and wouldn't get off until I was physically removed. I didn't cry, not once. There was no comfort. Prayers meant nothing to me, not now.

My father had introduced us all to his church, with which he was very involved and which we all used to attend. But once he died, I turned my back on it. Where was God? What sort of God would cut short the life of my father – a good Christian, a kind, hard-working person, a man who had done so much for the church? I became very angry: with God, with my mother, and with the whole world. Grief isn't fair-minded, it is an overwhelming pain that takes hold of you and keeps you in its grip until it's ready to let you go. You just have to wait it out. I didn't cry until a good year after Dad's death.

My mum must have done her crying alone – she never showed her grief to us kids. With Dad gone, she now had to work to support us and she started doing any jobs she could, including making tassels, which we would help her with at home. I decided that I needed to step into my father's shoes. I was the oldest child and I felt it was my responsibility to help provide for my siblings. As much as I loved my college course, I didn't think twice about giving it up and finding work. My dreams of being a performer were shelved. My family needed me.

One of the jobs I found was as a sales assistant in a shoe shop, but the manager was a creep, a sexual predator, always trying to look up my skirt when I went up a ladder to find a pair of shoes. My dad had always taught me to be careful around men, so I knew this was something I didn't have to put up with, which wasn't always the case for young women at that time. So I walked out of that job and didn't look back. Then, a lucky break. My mum had a cleaning job at the BBC and she got me an interview in the catering department. It wasn't just any old catering job, it was a supervisory role in hospitality, meaning I would be sorting out the food and drink for all the stars who were guests of the BBC.

Come the day of the interview, I was trying not to show my nerves. I had chosen my outfit carefully, a deep blue dress that flattered my figure without being too showy. Now all I had to do was to convince my potential new boss that I was up to the job.

"So, what experience can you bring to this role?" asked Alice, from the other side of the desk. A tall, thin woman with corkscrew curls, Alice had very twinkly green eyes and immediately put me at my ease.

"Well, I have been cooking since I was 10," I said. "Helping my mum in the kitchen, not just when she was preparing family meals but also when she catered for other people's parties."

"Have you had any supervisory experience?" asked Alice. I had to think fast. "Well, I have three younger siblings, who can be a bit of a handful," I ventured. Did I see a faint smile turning up the corners of Alice's mouth?

"Hospitality for celebrities can be quite challenging. Why do you think we should pick you rather than anyone else?" she asked.

"Well, I love my food so I know how important it is to get it right," I said, and Alice roared with laughter. I started work the following week.

From day one, I loved my job at the BBC. I enjoyed making sure that everything in the dining room was laid out beautifully for our guests and that they had everything they needed. Part of my role was to talk to the celebrities, to put them at their ease and to make sure that they were happy. I seemed to have a natural aptitude for this kind of work. I was fast, I was smart and it didn't harm that I was pretty. I also knew how to build a conversation, even with people who were at the top of the celebrity A-List. From London's best-loved comedians to world-famous actors, or the singer of the latest Bond theme, I was never intimidated by the stars that came into our dining room, but I was starstruck a couple of times. I think my most memorable guest was Muhammad Ali, who was huge in every way: his personality, his charisma, his physique. He was just gorgeous and despite his fame, he was so warm and friendly, making a point of talking to me.

"Do you have everything you need, Mr Ali?" I asked him as he stood at the buffet.

He stopped loading up his plate and turned to look at me. Believe me, when Muhammad Ali gives you his attention, you feel like the only other person in the world.

"What's your name?" He smiled.

"Amelia Nazario," I said, keeping my voice low and steady.

"Well, Amelia, everything is just wonderful, thank you," said the man who was one of my all-time heroes.

Spending so much time around world-famous stars, I was constantly reminded that kindness and courtesy always outshone fame and money. My dad, of course, could have told me that…

I had been working for a few months when I got the chance to find my own spotlight. My uncle had a reggae band with his daughters, my cousins, and they used to get quite a few gigs. My uncle knew I could sing, so when he asked me to join the band I leapt at the chance. Apart from my aching desire to perform, I also wanted to join as an act of rebellion. I knew full well my mum and dad would never have approved of me joining the band: this wasn't church music, it was pop music and, Heaven help us, it was all about showing off. In their eyes it was most certainly a sin, completely against their beliefs, and that was part of its appeal for me. I was still very angry – with my dad for leaving us, with my mum for just about everything else – and I needed an outlet for that grief-fuelled rage.

I loved everything about being on a stage: the lights, the glamour, the crowds. There was nothing like that anticipation backstage just before we were introduced, and the sheer thrill of going out there to an excited audience who wanted to love you. I felt beautiful, sassy and strong. In some ways, I think performing helped to calm and heal my ragged, broken heart.

The band was pretty successful, and we were performing all over the country. My uncle was very smart, good at connecting with the right people, at getting us gigs, getting us noticed. We even caught the interest of a music mogul, who invited us to his beautiful home overlooking the sea in Scandinavia. It was the first time I had ever encountered a toilet that flushed itself – a toilet that flushed itself? That was surely a measure of success, I thought to myself.

Whilst I loved singing harmonies with my cousins, they were becoming more commercial and going in a musical direction I didn't really like. It was time for me to stop being a backing singer and to go solo.

"Kimberly, can you go to the doctors and get me a sick note?"

Juggling my day job in BBC hospitality and my night job as a singer was tricky and sometimes required a bit of artful dodging. I now had a successful solo career, which sometimes meant going to Europe for a whole week. And so I would ask my sister Kimberly, who looks a bit like me, to get me a sick note, which would allow me to be away from work legitimately. Luckily, we were never caught out. It was a heady, exciting, exhausting time and I loved every minute of it. Once I left the band I seemed to go from strength to strength. I was gigging at prestigious places such as Ronnie Scott's and had some chart success, even appearing on 'Top of the Pops'. My day job actually helped my singing career because all the DJs at the BBC would plug my records. But once my catering managers got wind of what was happening, they tried to block the radio stations from playing me. I'm not really sure why, I suppose they wanted to keep me in my place and not blur the professional lines. But the DJs were my friends and would still promote my music at night, even if they couldn't do it in the daytime.

For a while, my mum was unaware of my other life as a singer, even though I was still living at home. I performed under a different name and I used to tell her that I was working a late shift or was seeing my cousins. When I came home from a gig, scrubbing off my make-up before I came through the front door, she was already tucked up in bed. By the time she found out, there was nothing much she could do about it, so she just let me get on with it.

While being on stage felt natural to me, I didn't take to the social side of the music business. All the other girls would give me a hard time for not joining in when they let their hair down. But I had been taught by my parents that it was a sin to smoke, a sin to drink and a sin to have boyfriends, so I didn't indulge in any of it. The hedonistic high life was not for me, partly because I wanted to honour the memory of my father, who would never have approved of such indulgence. Even in death, he was keeping me on the straight and narrow, which kept me safe. It also meant I was innocent and naïve...

3

THE COFFEE MACHINE

It all seems to happen in slow motion. I see him standing at the coffee machine. The same old, slightly beaten-up coffee machine I visit every day. Except today it looks different, it looks all shiny and new because he's standing next to it. I stop in my tracks as he slowly turns; it's as though he can suddenly feel my eyes blazing into his caramel skin. He holds my gaze, his jewelled hazel eyes dancing with… what? Interest? *Maybe.* Amusement? *Probably.* And something else, something deep and unfathomable, drawing me to him and inviting me in. My heart is pounding, my legs are unsteady, my hands clammy. *What is happening to me?* And where did he come from?

It was four years since I started at the BBC and I was very busy and happy. I had a great job, I loved singing in the evenings and I was able to help my mum support the family financially. Love was the last thing on my mind, yet it came and found me anyway. It had started as such an ordinary working day and began, as always, with coffee.

It was a morning pleasure I allowed myself only after I'd made sure everything was prepared for the day ahead. True, it was a slightly dubious pleasure, given the state of the beverage that came out of our machine, but I looked forward to it nonetheless. Sitting and enjoying my coffee was my little window of calm, a chance to take a deep breath before the busy shift ahead when I would rarely take a pause.

"The usual?" I asked Alice, who never said no to a coffee. "I think I'll have it black today," replied my boss. "I need a bit of a wake-up shot. How do you always manage to look fresh as a daisy?"

Well, it certainly wasn't early nights. I was often gigging with my music in the evening and not getting into bed until the early hours.

"Make-up!" I replied with a grin. I was only half-joking. From a young age I had always loved make-up and seemed to have a natural flair for it – I even wore it during those hairbrush concerts in my bedroom. I now had it down to a fine art, knowing exactly how to use it to accentuate my features and hide imperfections, like tired eyes. I always made sure I was well-groomed for my job at the BBC. Looking anything less than my best would have been deeply unprofessional.

"Oh by the way," said Alice, "the schedules may not run smoothly today. The electricity is down in the studio and there is work going on in there all day."

"Well it'll be worth the disruption if they finally sort out those electricity surges," I replied. My natural inclination to always look on the bright side was one of the things that Alice said she valued about me. We had such a good working relationship that my colleagues were always teasing me about being her favourite.

"And will you get some custard creams?" called Alice as I strode off to the coffee machine.

And that's when I first laid eyes on him. This man, this stranger, who stopped me in my tracks. I just saw his profile at first as he stood at the coffee machine. He was tall, about six foot two, with thick, silky black hair and a strong jaw. Even from that angle, he had my attention: it was as though there was an electric white light all the way around him. But then, he turned it up to full beam. Plastic cup in hand, he swung round and looked straight into my eyes. I felt as though someone had punched me in the gut.

Why am I shaking? How can a complete stranger make me nervous?

My thoughts were soon halted.

"Hello," he said, in a rich, deep voice. "I'm Logan." "Hello," I replied nervously, trying to keep breathing. "And you are…?" He flashed me a killer smile. "Amelia."

"Nice to meet you Amelia."

I could tell from his appearance that he was mixed heritage. And devastatingly handsome. *Can I touch your caramel skin?* I pulled myself together. "I guess from your uniform that you're an electrician?" I ventured.

"Clever, as well as beautiful." He smiled.

Trying to ignore the fireworks in my tummy, I said, "So, how long are you here for?"

"Should be about three months, give or take."

Oh good, time to get to know him. I managed to nod and collected my coffees, aware of his electric presence nearby.

"See you later," I said. *See you later? Really, Amelia, is that the best you could do?*

Feeling flustered, I walked away quickly, but Logan soon caught up with me.

"Amelia, when's your lunch break?" he asked softly. "It would be nice to get to know you."

"Sorry, I am in a hurry," I said, scurrying away as fast as I could. I didn't look back, but I knew he was looking at me as I dived into Alice's office, the hot coffee spilling out of the cups and burning my fingers.

"Nice chat?" smirked Alice, who had clearly seen the whole thing.

"His name is Logan and he's an electrician," I replied defensively.

"I hired him, I know who he is," smiled Alice, enjoying my obvious discomfort. "It was you who needed the information."

Barely suppressing her laughter, Alice turned away to her computer and all I could do was return to my own office next door.

I tried to make sense of the confusing storm of emotions within me. I had never felt like this before. What was going on? I was shaken to my core, my heart racing, my cheeks flushed. Surely this couldn't have been all on account of this one man… I had no experience of men so I didn't know what to do. Raised in a strict household, interaction with boys was never allowed. I was brought up to believe that any fraternising with the opposite sex was a sin, so I avoided it. Of course, I hadn't got to the age of 25 without receiving any male attention, but I always shrank away from it, my dad's warning words always ringing in my ears and sending me running as far away as I could from any romantic interest.

But I couldn't stop thinking about Logan. He was on my mind all that day and the next. Try as hard as I might to eliminate him from my thoughts, he'd just pop into them uninvited, sending my heart spinning into fifth gear. I felt thrilled and afraid at the same time. I didn't know what to do with these feelings and I was finding it hard to concentrate. "And then the elephant sat on my knee and ate the dandelion…" said Alice.

"Yes – what? What elephant?" I didn't have a clue what she was talking about.

"Just testing. Amelia, you haven't been listening to a word I've said for the past five minutes," smiled Alice.

"Sorry, I was a bit distracted."

"Hmm, wouldn't have anything to do with the lovely Logan, would it?" she said, knowingly. "He must be a good electrician because he certainly created some sparks between you."

While Alice laughed at her own joke, my cheeks burned hot. "Just need to go and check the tables," I muttered, as I hurried away.

Unable to deal with whatever Logan had stirred up, I decided the best thing to do was simply avoid him. And this proved quite easy to do. If I were ever needed to attend the offices near the main studio where he was working, I would simply send someone else. My avoidance strategy worked for two weeks. If I was disappointed that he hadn't come to seek me out, I wasn't going to admit it to myself.

"So, what's the story with the lovely Logan?" asked Alice one afternoon.

"Nothing, no nothing," I stammered. "I haven't even seen him about the place."

"Well, from the way you were both devouring one another with your eyes on that first day, I thought you'd have been engaged by now," laughed Alice. "Or at the very least had a date or two. Why haven't you?"

Because I have no experience of men. Because I'm scared by the power of my feelings. Because he hasn't come to find me.

Then, one day, he did. Lunchtimes in the staff canteen were always hectic, especially since the new Caribbean chef had updated the menu. It was usually a sociable meal, as TV and radio employees would join together for a communal lunch.

I was just tucking into some succulent fried fish when I heard a voice that sent a tingle down my spine.

"Do you mind if I join you?"

I looked over my right shoulder to see Logan standing behind me, an irresistible grin on his face. He was holding a bottle of lemonade in his left hand and in the other, a plate of jerk chicken and chips.

"N-no," I managed to stumble out.

He sat down next to me and I could feel the heat of his forearm next to mine on the table.

"I've not seen you in a while, have you been away?" he asked.

"No, I've been here." *Hiding from you.*

"Well it's great to see you again." He smiled that devastating smile. "Tell me about yourself, Amelia."

He remembers my name. "What do you want to know?" "Everything."

He was a good listener, hanging on to my every word and offering an encouraging question that made me open up even more. I found myself telling him about my life outside work, about my hobbies, my love of the arts. Even as my words poured out, I was dimly aware of my father's voice at the back of my mind. "Amelia, you must be a strong, successful, independent woman. Don't rely on men for anything. Whatever you do, keep them at arm's length." I stopped talking finally, aware that I had shared too much.

"Is that the time?" I said, glancing at the canteen clock. "I have to get back, so nice to see you again. Bye." I didn't let him get a word in edgeways, as I shot up from the table and attempted another quick getaway. Then I felt a warmth engulf my right palm. Never in my life had a man held my hand. And it was happening right now, in the middle of the canteen, with all its echoing chatter and clatter. His hand in mine felt good, his skin the perfect soft and rough ratio. *Keep breathing, Amelia.*

"Could we perhaps have lunch again, outside of work?" said Logan.

Yes, yes, a million times yes. "As much as I'd like to, I have to remain on the premises in case my boss Alice needs me," I said, conscious that his hand was still folded around mine. "It's my responsibility to attend to the celebrities should something crop up. How about we meet here again tomorrow?"

"Sure," smiled Logan. "Same time, same place."

I picked up my bag and, as I left the canteen, felt as though I was floating a few inches above the ground. My world had stopped when he had put his hand in mine. With that one touch, he had given me a feeling of such calm and safety. How was that even possible? My hand was still tingling, all my senses in shock. I was still reliving the moment at home that evening. My emotions were whirling around, and I could barely sit still. I started to think that perhaps it was a bad idea to meet Logan the following day.

I am walking up the aisle and I can see my groom waiting for me at the altar. As he turns around to look at his bride, his eyes are shining with love. Logan's bright hazel eyes...

It wasn't unusual for me to fantasise about being a bride. I would often create in my mind the perfect wedding, me in my perfect white dress with a cathedral train, the groom in his black tailored suit. Usually, the groom's face wasn't defined, it would just appear as a bright light, without any features. But as I lay on my bed that night, the face of the imaginary man was etched out clearly in my mind for the first time ever.

No! That's impossible. I've only met Logan for lunch once. How has he suddenly become my fantasy husband?

I did not feel ready for the strength of these emotions. I realised I needed to put up some firm protective barriers.

Despite my fears, I met Logan for lunch in the canteen the following day and every day after that for the whole week. I remembered, when I was younger, someone once said to me that you can tell if a boy likes you because when you are with him you feel good about yourself. Logan was full of praise for my beauty, my personality, and he made me feel so special that I could only hope he shared my growing feelings. He shared his own stories with me too, and I learned that he was a confident, affectionate man who was an only child and very close to his mum. He didn't have any sort of relationship with his father, who sounded like a controlling man. I also discovered that his favourite sport was cricket and that he loved all sorts of music. At 29, he was four years older than me.

With each day that passed, I could feel my worries melting away, my barriers lowering as our knowledge and understanding of one another deepened. We shared so many things: a love of music, of being in the spotlight, an ambition to make the best of ourselves. He was so warm, so charming and he knew how to make me laugh. My father's words of warning became so faint that I couldn't really hear them anymore.

A month passed and as usual I looked forward to our precious lunchtimes. On this particular day, Logan arrived with his meal readily prepared, as usual, so as not to waste valuable conversation time.

"So, are you single or dating?" he asked, completely out of the blue.

I almost choked on my food and slowly put down my fork. Suddenly, that feeling of dread returned. As long as we were just meeting for lunch, it was fine, I was safe. Part of me didn't feel ready to turn our relationship into something else, another part of me was aching to take us to a romantic place. But I had no experience to draw on and I was frightened of getting out of my depth.

"Single and not dating," I said finally, hoping he hadn't noticed my blushing cheeks.

"Well in that case, and if you would allow me, I would love to take you out," said Logan.

"On a date?" *Amelia, what a stupid question, of course he means a date.*

"Yes, on a date." There was that killer smile again. I said yes, of course.

However, there would be no date if Logan didn't get my mum's approval. So, before he drove round to pick me up, I did my best to pave the way. My mother Florence was a very discerning woman, so I made sure to paint Logan in the best light possible, telling her only the things I thought she would like to hear. "He really loves him mum and has a great relationship with her – I tease him sometimes about it and call him a mummy's boy," I enthused. "He always says he would do anything for her." Florence just sat and listened, saying nothing, revealing nothing on her face. No matter what I said, she would decide for herself, thank you very much. Logan's charm would cut no ice with my mother, but I just hoped she would see the good things I saw in him.

I took hours getting ready, trying to ignore the butterflies in my tummy. I had chosen to wear a baby pink pencil dress that hugged my curves and I made sure my hair was curled perfectly and looking its glossy best. Make-up done, heels on, a final lick of lipstick and I was good to go. I surveyed myself in the mirror. *You'll do.*

"There's someone at the door!" bellowed Kimberly from her perch at the bay window in the front room. "Kimberly, get away from the window!"

My dad always said, "Amelia, if a man arrives at your home to take you anywhere, and beeps the horn to announce his arrival, don't go out to meet him. A proper gentleman leaves his vehicle and knocks on the door." Or rings the bell. Ding-dong! The chimes rang through the house. My stomach did a somersault. Here he was then, no backing out now...

4

CHANGING ROTAS

I am walking slowly up the aisle, listening to the organ music, seeing the smiling faces of my friends, my brother, my sisters. My mum. I can smell the sweet fragrance of my bouquet and the fresh flowers forming a guard of honour at the end of each pew. There's a reassuring presence walking beside me – my dad? I feel calm, happy, all fears and doubts silenced by the sure, steady beat of my heart. I am marrying my one true love. I see him up ahead, waiting for me, and I am full of joy and gratitude. As I get closer, I see there is another figure at the altar. The sequins on her wedding dress catch the sunlight as she moves closer to the groom, her long veil hiding her face. They both turn their backs on me. The sound of my own voice, screaming, wakes me up. *It was just a dream, Amelia, a nightmare, it's not real...*

The meeting of two worlds. The door opened and the

cold outside air met the warm atmosphere of home. From the top of the stairs I could see Logan framed in the doorway, beaming his bright, confident smile. Despite my nerves, I couldn't help noticing that he looked gorgeous in his dark brown leather jacket and flared jeans. If he was surprised to see my mother standing there instead of me, he hid it well.

"Pleased to meet you, I'm Logan," he said, offering his hand.

My mother stood, rigid-backed, with one hand on her hip and the other on the doorknob. Though I couldn't see her face, her body language told me that her expression was stern, and I knew she would be scrutinising Logan from the crown of his black hair to the tips of his leather noir shoes. I felt sure there was a welcome smile on her tightly pressed lips. "Mrs Na-za-rio," she said frostily, offering her fingertips to shake. "Come and wait in the front room."

Anxious to rescue Logan from whatever discomfort my mother had in store for him, I came downstairs and could see Logan standing just inside the half-closed door.

Oh no, that is not a good sign.

As I pushed open the door fully, I noticed with dismay that my hands were trembling. My mother was sitting on the only single lounge chair in the front room. I knew what she was up to. Being the canny, intuitive woman that she was, she had purposely not invited Logan to sit to see if he would move of his own accord. I wasn't sure whether, by not sitting, Logan had failed or passed Mum's test.

"Hi Logan," I said, breaking the heavy silence. "Hello Amelia." He smiled warmly at me.

My mother fixed me with her beady eye and ordered me

to follow her into the kitchen. Knowing that this did not bode well, I told Logan to wait for me in the car and I almost smiled at the relief on his face. In the kitchen, however, Florence was not smiling. I knew this look only too well.

"How much do you know about this man, Amelia?"

"Quite a lot, Mum. He is an only child, he loves cricket-"

"You know only what he has told you, so really you know nothing," she interrupted. Before I could reply, Florence carried on. "He's not the one for you. His atmosphere and presence don't seem right."

"He's really nice at work and popular with all the staff-" "What do you know about his past? Has he had many girlfriends?"

"I don't know, Mum."

"And marriage, has he ever been married? Any children?"

"I – don't think so," I said, without much conviction.

"Answers you do not know, Amelia, because of questions you have not asked."

She was right of course, I hadn't asked, but why on earth would I ask him such questions? I was far too shy to ask him about his romantic past, and anyway, that wasn't the sort of thing we talked about. What did it matter anyway, when we clearly only had eyes for one another? I was puzzled by Mum's attitude and a little upset. But I had to remind myself that Mum didn't know Logan as I did and that she was only looking out for my interests, just as my dad would have done. Even so, I was anxious to end the conversation and worried about what Logan was thinking as he sat out in the car. Mum finally noticed my constant glances towards the front door.

"Go," she said at last. It wasn't approval, but at least I had her permission.

In the car, Logan was tapping his fingers on the steering wheel in time to the music on the radio.

If he asks me, I'm going to have to lie.

"Are you okay?" he said. "Yes, I'm fine."

Please don't ask me what she said.

"What did your mum say? Did I get her stamp of approval?"

Here goes. "Yes, she liked you." *Just a little white lie.*

We spent the rest of the journey in silence, the radio filling in the gaps where the conversation should have been. He had booked a very exclusive, five-star restaurant in the West End. I was impressed. Through my music world, I knew quite a lot about fine wining and dining. Logan had chosen well. After the awkward beginning to our date, we could now, finally, take a deep breath, sink into the plush velvet seats and relax.

"One glass of red and one of white, please. Then may I have a steak, well done, and for the lady, salmon."

Hang on, Logan, don't I get a say in what I eat? I knew social etiquette required the man to order the food, but surely only after his date had actually chosen what she wanted? And white wine? I was used to champagne. Then I felt guilty for having such ungracious thoughts. I could see that Logan was doing his best to make it a special first date.

The conversation soon flowed between us and became deeper with each delicious course. Every now and then I heard my mother's words: "Answers you do not know, Amelia, because of questions you have not asked." But I silenced the little niggle of doubt she had placed in my mind.

I was enjoying getting closer to Logan and wasn't about to spoil what turned out to be a wonderful evening.

"How was your weekend, Amelia?" asked Alice the following Monday.

"Great thanks."

"Do anything special?"

"Well if you call a date with Logan special," I said, unable to suppress my huge grin.

"And about time too! How was it?"

"Great. Brilliant. We had dinner in the West End."

"He sounds like a keeper," said Alice. "But hold it right there. We need coffee, then I want to hear all about it, every single detail."

"A lady doesn't kiss and tell." I smiled. "Oh, so there was kissing then?"

"I'll get you that coffee, Alice."

"And don't forget the custard creams, it's the least you can do if you're not going to share!" Alice shouted after me.

Over the next eight weeks, Logan and I grew closer and closer. Lunch after lunch, date after date, our relationship blossomed. One night, when Logan introduced me to friends with the words, "This is my girlfriend Amelia," I thought I would burst with happiness. He showed me off as if I were a precious crown jewel, and he certainly made me feel valued. Logan was so attentive, always showering me with gifts and flowers. He was supportive of my music and loved to watch me perform, slotting perfectly into that glamorous world. We went to the cinema, ate at restaurants all over London, enjoyed river cruises on the Thames and so much more. I was giddy with the romantic excitement of it all. I was a novice when it came to relationships with men, but I couldn't imagine that anything could have felt better, more right than this. We had such a strong connection with one another, and it only intensified with each day that passed.

The only slightly dark cloud on my horizon was knowing that the work on the main studio was coming to an end and, with Logan starting a contract with another local business, our lunch dates wouldn't be quite so easy to arrange.

"My lunch hour will be different to yours," said Logan. "So I will only get to see you for about 10 minutes before I have to head back."

"That's a shame, we'll just have to meet after work then," I replied, not ready for what he said next.

"Or you could just move in with me," he said, chuffed with himself for coming up with such a great idea.

My horrified face must have been a picture. "We can't do that!" I gasped. "We're not married. Plus we've only been seeing one another for a couple of months."

What would Mum say? This goes against everything my parents have ever taught me.

"Amelia, you don't have to be married to live together. This is the 20th century, not the dark ages."

"Let me think about it," I said. Seeing the pleased gleam in Logan's eyes, I warned, "I can't guarantee my answer will be yes. This is a huge decision for me."

Once I got home, I spent hours pondering what to do. My mother wouldn't countenance such a move, seeing it as a sin to be living as man and wife without a wedding ring. Old fashioned it may have been by current standards, but it was a deeply held belief from which she would never be swayed.

Mum was certain that she had God on her side when it came to matters such as these. And I knew that my dad would have agreed with her, too. As for me, I knew that living with Logan would be a dream come true. *And then eventually we could get married, so everything would be fine.* I went round and round in circles, torn between Logan and my mother. Whatever I decided, one of them would be upset with me.

The telephone interrupted my thoughts.

"Have you told your mum yet?" asked Logan eagerly. "Do you need me to come and collect your things?"

"No, Logan, I told you I need time," I said in a hushed voice, afraid my mum would get the gist of the conversation.

"Well if you have to think about it, you can't really love me," he said heatedly.

"Logan, it's not just me I have to think about, there's my whole family. I'm the eldest and I have responsibilities now that Dad's gone. Who will help Mum if I'm not here?"

I held my breath, waiting for his response. It came in the form of a monotonous beep, telling me he had hung up the phone. I didn't sleep a wink that night, wondering if I had just put an end to our relationship. The following morning Logan called and asked me to meet him after work. I agreed. I still hadn't decided what I was going to do, but I needed to know what was going through Logan's mind – even if I didn't like what it was.

The day seemed endless. I was jumpy and worried about our meeting, wondering if it would be the last time I would see Logan. I concentrated on work to take my mind off the disaster I imagined was waiting for me at the end of the day.

Logan was leaning on his car, waiting for me. Smiling,

he opened the passenger door and I slid into the seat with a lifted heart. *Perhaps it's going to be all right.* But my hopes were soon dashed. As I chatted away nervously about how my day had been and asked him about his, Logan didn't say a word. Instead of answering my questions, he focused on the road ahead, his jaw clenched.

Why won't he talk to me? Is he angry with me? And where are we going?

Thankfully the journey was short and the awkward silence was broken by the sound of tyres grinding against gravel as we pulled into the car park of a nature reserve. We walked in silence, tension fizzing between us, until we reached a bridge overlooking a tranquil lake. My heart, by contrast, was jumping all over the place. I wanted to cry, I wanted to reach out to him and say, "I'm sorry, let's just go back to how we were. Please don't be like this." But I said nothing. I was at a loss.

Finally he said, "Amelia, I have strong feelings for you and I think – hope – you feel the same. Being with you these last two months has shown me how much I need you in my life and only being able to see you when schedules allow is too hard for me. I think our relationship is perfect and I think living together would be the start of building our whole lives together."

I felt a surge of relief and happiness. This was an outpouring of love, a promise of sorts. *The beginning of our lives together.* I hadn't been looking for love but here it was anyway, and it felt so right. When I looked back at our time together so far, it wasn't such a huge leap to think about a happy future together. And his words made me realise he was serious about me. Living with him, being together all the time, would be a dream come true. Money wouldn't be an issue because we were both in good jobs. And it would be the first step to getting married.

"I feel the same way too," I said carefully. "But let me think it through and work out how best to sort it out. Then I'll let you know, okay?"

Although clearly disappointed that I hadn't jumped for joy at his declaration, Logan agreed to leave it to me. Why didn't I jump for joy? The major reason was waiting for me at home. Until I had taken the plunge and told my mum, I couldn't even begin to believe that my dream would come true.

Once I got home, I decided to test out the waters with my mother. Hopefully, she would understand that Logan just wanted to sort out our living arrangements before he proposed.

Florence was sitting in the garden, watching the sunset and humming one of her favourite tunes. Catching her in a mellow moment was the perfect opportunity.

"Mum, I've got something to tell you."

"Oh, what is that?" Florence replied, blissfully unaware of anything but her joyful humming.

"Logan has asked me to move in with him."

Florence's blissed-out mood disappeared with the sun and a mask of rage covered her face.

"I asked you once and I'll ask you again, Amelia: exactly what do you know about him and how do you think it is possible to move into a man's home *when you are not married?*"

I had no words to reply to that. I knew my mum was right, I just didn't know what I could do about it. I went to bed that night feeling agitated and conflicted. Torn between the expectations of the man I adored and my mother's values, I fell into a restless sleep.

The next morning brought more clarity and I arranged to meet Logan after work. It was a sunny evening and I suggested a walk around the city rather than getting into the car.

We hadn't got very far when I got right to the point. "Logan, is there anything in your past that you think I should know about?"

"My past?" he said, taken aback. "Like what? I'm not an ex-convict if that's what you're worried about." He chuckled, but was clearly wondering where this was going.

"No, I mean previous relationships," I said, unable to look him in the eye. "I mean, you must have had girlfriends in the past. Or maybe you were married before?"

"Yes but – no…" He was fidgeting nervously.

A cold wave washed over me. "Married? Have you been married?"

We stopped strolling as I awaited his reply.

"Yes, but it's over. Totally over," he said, his voice strained. "Are you still married? Do you live together?"

"We live in the same house but we are apart. We live separate lives."

I'm not hearing this, it's a bad dream. "So you're a married man?" The voice coming out of my mouth didn't sound like me.

"No, separated."

"Right, well, I'm going to miss my train." I fled towards the nearest underground, feeling sick and confused. *So Mum was right. He's married!! How can he be married? How could he lie to me? This is the end, I can't ever see him again now.*

My heart physically ached as I lay in bed that night. How could I have been so foolish as to believe all his honeyed words? I knew I was an innocent when it came to men, but this seemed like a very harsh lesson indeed. How would I ever trust a man again? I eventually cried myself to sleep.

I was glad that the rain was lashing down the next day. It mirrored my stormy mood exactly.

"You look as if you had a late one, Amelia," smiled Alice when I deposited her coffee on her desk. "Out partying with your boyfriend again?"

Unable to contain the well of sadness inside me, I burst into floods of tears. Alice gently closed her office door and led me to a seat. "What happened?"

"It's too long a story, we have to get ready for the first guests," I blubbed.

"Don't you worry about that," soothed Alice. "We have all the time you need. Now, tell me."

So I did. I told her the whole story.

"Well it's not the end of the world," said Alice, when I had finished.

"How can you say that? He's a married man."

"No, he's in a broken marriage and probably living with his spouse for financial reasons," said Alice. "This sort of thing happens all the time. Heck, I should know, I started dating when I was divorcing you-know-who." She took a tissue from the box on her desk and wiped the tears running down my face. "Now cheer up, take a breath and give him a call."

Back at my desk, I pondered what Alice had said. I smiled to think about my boss being my relationship counsellor. Alice herself admitted that, when it came to men, she had 'an unfailing knack of picking wrong 'uns' and she had many a story about her dating disasters. But, unlike me, she did at least have experience to draw on. Was she right? Was I making a fuss about nothing?

I finally plucked up the courage to call Logan. He sounded very happy and relieved to hear from me. We chatted about this and that for a while. As I listened to the sound of his voice, I became certain about what I needed to do.

"Logan, after yesterday, I think it's best if we take a break from one another. I can't date a married man."

"Does that mean we're over forever?"

"While you're married, yes."

"But I'm getting a divorce, I'm doing all the paperwork now. Can we still speak on the phone while it's going through?"

"Only on the phone. I'm not meeting you or seeing you until it's final. Bye, Logan."

I hung up the phone, took my pocket mirror from my handbag and refreshed my lipstick. Then, with a deep breath, I walked out of my office and started my working day.

5

LONDON UNDERGROUND

The audience whoops as I finish my song and I can feel tears stinging my eyes. Why is it that nearly all of the numbers I perform are about love? I feel as if I am telling my own life story right up here on this stage: the joy of love found, the agony of love lost. I have never sung with such raw emotion and the audience can feel that it's authentic. I feel such gratitude for their warm applause and such delight to be standing there, that for a second, I forget. I look over to where he would normally be, clapping proudly, but he's not there. *Keep it together, Amelia, just a couple more.* I summon my biggest smile and nod to the musicians. The show, as they say, must go on.

Five long months passed and the only contact I had with Logan was the couple of phone calls we shared every week. I went to work at the BBC, I did my singing gigs at night, the same as I always had. But everything seemed different now. I hadn't realised how quickly and profoundly he'd been woven into the fabric of my life. It wasn't just his physical presence – at my gigs, at lunch or dinner, on a day out somewhere – that I missed. It was the constant joy I had felt at knowing that we were together, the looking forward to the next time, the sparkle my life had gained with him by my side.

There were so many times during those five months that I had wanted to call him and say, "I miss you, come and get me." But I resisted. I could only be with Logan if he were a free man. How could I ever rejoice in our love if it was based on a sin? Our weekly phone calls were usually strained, our chitchat papering over the real questions that I wanted to ask. *Are you divorced yet?* Then, any tender moment between us would make me miss him all the more. I dreaded those calls as much as I looked forward to them. Then came a phone call that changed everything.

"Hi, it's me."

"Hello Logan, how are you?"

"The divorce has been finalised," he said. "I've moved out of the house and into my own flat. Just me."

I can't believe it, could this really be happening? I couldn't speak, my heart was so full.

"Amelia, are you still there? Did you hear what I just said? Look, these last few months have been the hardest, not being able to see you, to hold you in my arms. I realise that I just can't be without you, Amelia. I – I love you."

Did he really just say those words? I love you? I LOVE YOU?

"I'm so glad you kept your promise, Logan. I can't be

without you either…" *Go on say it!* "I love you too."

We both gave a delighted, child-like giggle. I felt the same warmth I had experienced when he first held my hand. After professing our love, we arranged to meet at Logan's new flat that evening.

I hadn't told my mother anything about what had gone on between me and Logan. She may have noticed a change in me over the last few months, but she never said a word. How could I now tell her that I was off to see the man she didn't like and the flat that I might move into with him? I did the only sensible thing in the circumstances – I lied.

"I'm going out with Alice tonight to talk over some work things."

"Don't work things happen at work?" said Florence, with her usual forensic ability to sniff out an untruth.

"Mainly yes, but we've found it's better to be out of the office when we brainstorm ideas." For someone who rarely told lies, I was becoming quite the expert. I still couldn't look my mum in the eye though.

The tube journey to Logan's new place was over in a flash. As I tip-tapped along the pavement in my stilettoes, I began to regret turning down his offer of a lift. But I didn't want our first meeting after five months to be outside a tube station, I wanted to make an entrance! Logan had given me detailed instructions on how to get there and I soon found the pleasant, tree-lined street he had directed me to. My heart was pounding as I rang the bell. Would we still have that same easy connection with one another, or would it be awkward after all this time apart?

I needn't have worried. Logan opened the door with a big

grin on his face and opened his arms wide.

"Welcome!" he said, before enveloping me in a strong hug.

"Hi Logan," I whispered into his neck.

He held me at arm's length and looked into my eyes for a moment, saying nothing. "Come on in," he said finally, taking my coat. "Go and take a look around and I'll meet you in the kitchen."

The living room had a co-ordinated cream and grey colour scheme. With its plush three-seat sofa, smoked glass coffee table and damask rug, it had the sort of smart but unlived-in showroom look that you might find in the home department of John Lewis. Just as I was imagining myself curled up on the sofa with Logan, the pop of a champagne cork drew me into the kitchen.

Modern and sleek, the kitchen featured marble work surfaces, the same grey and cream colour scheme and I was guessing that there were state-of-the-art integrated appliances behind the glossy cabinet doors.

"I hope you don't mind but I thought I'd cook rather than us going out tonight," said Logan, pulling out a chair for me at the dining table. The scene was set for a romantic dinner: a table set for two, with candles and a bottle of champagne chilling on ice, soulful ballads playing on the hi-fi. And, as he started to serve, I could see that tonight's menu was a glistening baked sea bass accompanied by Lyonnaise potatoes.

"I just wish you'd gone to a bit of trouble," I said in a deadpan voice.

Logan's startled face turned to me, then when he saw me

giggling, he collapsed into laughter, too.

"Well, it's an important night," he said.

"It all looks beautiful," I said as I watched him move agilely around the kitchen, adding the finishing touches to our delicious-looking meal. "Thanks for doing this and thanks for keeping your promise. I have missed you so much and now, being here, it feels as if we have never been apart."

"I told you I was making arrangements to be with you and only you," he said. "It all took longer than planned but now it's done and there's no need for us to speak of it again. Let's just look forward now."

He placed a gold-rimmed white china plate in front of me and sat down opposite. Then he poured us each a glass of champagne in delicate flutes.

"To us?" He smiled.

I tapped my glass against his. "To us."

We spent the next few hours sharing stories of what had happened during the past five months. We agreed that the stories would have been entirely different had we still been together. Then we agreed that we never wanted to be apart again. Talk turned inevitably to the next step.

"The answer's yes," I said. "I've had plenty of time to think about it and you've shown me your commitment to our relationship. So, yes, I will move in."

Logan's eyes shone with happiness. "Let me know when and I'll come to pick up all your things."

We sealed the deal with a gentle clink of our glasses.

In the taxi home that night, I decided that I wouldn't prolong the agony at home. I would tell Florence the following day and move out straight away. I wasn't looking forward to it.

I awoke, as I did every Saturday morning, to the smell of Mum's breakfast and the sound of Jaden and Zoe's lively playing. When I realised this could be the last Saturday I would ever wake up in my childhood home, I felt a little melancholy. All those happy memories, especially of when my dad was alive. But I also knew it was time to go. I rehearsed various ways of dropping the bombshell, but I couldn't think of any version that wouldn't end with my mum exploding.

"Amelia, breakfast!" came the call from below. I took a deep breath.

I always loved our weekend breakfasts, everyone sitting around the table together, chatting and laughing, as we enjoyed Florence's delicious cooking. Breakfast was over before I knew it. As the oldest sibling, it was my responsibility to help Mum clear up once we had finished eating and I figured this was my best chance to break the news.

"Mum, Logan has asked me to move in with him as we will be getting married," I said, my arms elbow deep in soapy water.

Florence looked at me in disbelief. "Marriage? What, out of thin air?"

"Not thin air, Mum. He wants to marry me and says it's best if we live together first as it sorts our living situation before we are married."

"You told me this five months ago. So why didn't you do it then? Why the delay? You were very keen."

There was no evading my mother, the truth bloodhound, once she was on the scent. "I had to wait on some things to be sorted out," I said.

"What things?" She practically threw the dishes on the table. "Did you get a mortgage with him?"

"No." I didn't like the dangerous look in my mother's eye.

"Did you save money with him?"

"No."

"What then? What are you hiding, Amelia? SPEAK!" Her tone switched from investigation to infuriation.

"I was waiting for his divorce to be final."

There was a deathly silence.

What have I just said? I'm a dead woman. She's going to kill me.

"Divorced?" Florence finally bellowed. "DIVORCED? You mean when you brought him into my house he was a *married* man? After everything your father and I taught you. Are you trying to disgrace me?"

"No, Mum, I didn't know," I said, tears streaming down my face.

"You didn't know? What do you mean? If you don't start explaining yourself, young lady, all hell is going to break loose in this house!"

"Well, after you told me I should find out more about him, I followed your advice. I was as shocked as you that he was married and told him he had to get a divorce before we could see one another again. So he did. Now he's single and has asked me to move in with him before we get married." I silently pleaded with my mother to understand. *Just for once, Mum, can you bend even the tiniest bit?*

"You're moving out," she said flatly.

"Well, you said I couldn't live with a man unless I was

married, and since we are going to be married, it's okay, isn't it?"

"Now you're using my own words against me," cried Florence. "Well, remember these words just like you remembered all my others: if you leave this house, don't you ever come back!"

"Fine! I'm never coming back!" I ran upstairs in floods of tears and began throw my things haphazardly into bags. I called Logan from the landing phone, my breath still ragged from the sobs that had been wracking through me. "Hold on, Amelia, I'm coming for you," was all he said before hanging up.

I managed not to cry when I kissed my sisters and brother goodbye. I felt so wretched – they all so looked upset and bewildered. When would I see those familiar, beloved faces again? I didn't know where my mother was as I walked out of the door and got into Logan's car. As we drove away I saw her silhouette behind the net curtains of the bay window, the same window through which Kimberly had watched Logan arrive for our first date. I wondered what was going through Florence's mind as she watched her eldest daughter leave home.

We didn't speak in the car. Every now and then, Logan would lay his hand on top of mine for a moment, the warmth of his touch calming the sobs still shuddering through me. I spent most of that night replaying the argument with my mum. I had never seen her so angry. 'Don't you ever come back' had been her final words to me and I knew that she meant it. I knew my mother; there would be no thawing over time, no softening.

How could she love me if she could say that to me? I have no mother now, no brother or sisters.

These unhappy thoughts haunted me for a few days, and I felt as if I was grieving for my family, just as I grieved for my dad. One evening, Logan found me sitting crying in the dark and put his arms around me.

"I've lost them all, Logan," I sobbed. "I've lost everyone."

"No you haven't," he said. "You've got me and I'm going to look after you. Your mum obviously didn't want to see you happy – why else would she have said what she did?" He kissed my nose. "Now, I'm going to run you a bath."

"Thank you, darling."

I sat in the bubbles and tried to relax, but my thoughts kept returning to my mother's words. She hadn't liked Logan from day one and never gave him a chance. Normally such an insightful judge of people's characters, how could Florence have got it so wrong this time? Logan was right, she didn't want me to be happy. She probably only wanted me to stay for the money I contributed to the house.

I need to stop dwelling on what I can't change and start to enjoy my new life. I owe it to Logan – and to myself.

For the next few months Logan was true to his word, and looked after me like a princess. He was so loving and supportive of everything I did, in and out of work. We wined and dined regularly, always finding new restaurants to try, as well as returning to our special favourites. Knowing my love of travel, he took me to Paris and Seville, treated me to a luxury spa weekend and was planning bigger, more far-flung trips in the future. He also indulged my passion for the theatre: we went to all the big openings of West End musicals and plays, where I would buy programmes to keep as a memento of our wonderful nights out together. We were inseparable, we were smitten, we were in love and perfect together. What could possibly go wrong?

6

GRAVITY-DEFYING PASTA

My finger is bleeding and I wrap some kitchen towel around it to staunch the flow. The bleach will sting if it goes anywhere near my cut, but I have to keep going. *Don't you dare stop, Amelia, not until it's all cleaned up.* I survey the mess on the walls and floor: pasta and chicken are mashed into the carpet, pieces of broken porcelain scattered everywhere. I try not to cry as I slowly, carefully clear away the debris. *It's as though I am throwing away my shattered dreams.* I start to scrub away at the stains, needing to remove all traces of the nightmare. *I had cherished such high hopes – where did it all go wrong?* I hear some movement upstairs and I quicken my frantic scrubbing.

My happy bubble burst on a bright day in early summer. After weeks of rain, the sun had finally come out and there was a promise of warmer days ahead, which is ironic really, because it was also the day when I was first shut out in the cold by the man I loved.

My workload at the BBC had doubled, reminding me that it was definitely the start of our busiest season, when artists around the UK would release tracks in an unspoken race to be summer's number one. Much as I loved my job, the summer season would leave me exhausted at the end of each hectic day. What kept me going was the thought of going home to Logan.

"Are you up for some overtime tonight?" asked Alice.

"Sorry, I don't think I'd be much good tonight, Alice, I'm all in."

Some things were more precious than money. I was looking forward to a chilled evening, a nice meal and making plans for our weekend. I was excited, as ever, to turn the corner into our street but surprised to see that Logan's car wasn't in its parking spot. He usually got home before me, particularly when our busy days required me to stay a little longer at work.

I was sitting in the lounge, wondering if he'd got stuck in traffic, when I heard his key in the lock.

"Hi darling, you're late today. Are you okay?"

"Hello," murmured Logan in response.

He sounded odd and when I went into the hallway, I saw that his face looked different, too. "Has something happened?"

He said nothing at all as he went upstairs. I would normally have followed him up and chatted to him as he showered and washed away the day. But this time I stayed downstairs. I was confused, I just couldn't understand why he was acting so strangely. I couldn't think of anything I'd done that could have upset him. Maybe something had happened at work. Then I heard him singing in the shower. Logan could not sing a note but I had never been more pleased to hear his flat, tuneless vocals. He was obviously back to his usual self. Encouraged by his shower performance, I met him as he came out of the bathroom.

But Logan didn't acknowledge me. Instead, he went to the wardrobe and took out a long-sleeved navy-blue shirt and his tailored black trousers.

"Are you going out?"

"Yes," he said curtly.

I don't understand. Why is he being so cold? And where is he going without me, in his smart clothes?

"Where are you going?" My voice betrayed none of the anxiety I was feeling. Receiving no reply, I repeated the question. Logan continued getting ready, apparently oblivious to me.

"What?" he finally snapped at me.

"Is everything okay?"

"Yes," he said, shutting down our minimalist conversation as he headed out of the bedroom. He collected his car keys from the side table and headed out through the front door.

"What time will you be– " The loud slam cut short my question.

I felt stung by Logan's behaviour and more than a little confused. *He must have had a bad day and doesn't want to take it out on me, so he's gone out to work it off.*

I wasn't entirely convinced by my reasoning, but couldn't think of any other reason for his abrupt behaviour. Assuming

Logan would be out for dinner, I cooked a solitary meal and tried to distract my restless mind with the TV. A few hours had passed without me hearing from Logan and since he would never stay out so late without calling, I tried his mobile. It went straight to voicemail. Presuming he had a bad reception, I tried again, with no luck. I turned back to the TV, trying to ignore my rising anxiety.

Just before midnight I tried him again; this time the phone rang but Logan declined the call. Trying not to worry, I went to bed, set my alarm and eventually fell into a light sleep, one ear listening out for his foot on the stairs. It was the first time I had gone to sleep on my own in my new home.

A muffled thump broke through my dreams and alerted me to the front door being banged shut. The bedside clock told me it was 3am. The smell of alcohol announced his arrival in the bedroom, and he stumbled around before finally dragging back the sheets and falling heavily into bed, bashing into me in the process. I remained still, holding the sheet tight over my shoulder, keeping my eyes firmly closed. Something told me I didn't want to confront whatever was in the room with me at that moment. He fell asleep instantly, his snores bouncing around the bedroom, but I lay wide-eyed for a long time.

The following morning, I awoke to see Logan's work clothes laid out over his side of the bed.

He's up early considering he only went to bed four hours ago.

"Did you have a good night with the boys?" I called through to the en-suite bathroom, where I could hear him cleaning his teeth.

He spat into the sink. "Don't question me," he snarled.

What is this? What is happening?

I walked into the en-suite and faced him. "Logan, what's the matter?"

"I said don't question me," he replied sharply, wiping his mouth.

Trying to lighten the mood, I raised my hand, like a child in a classroom trying to get the teacher's attention. "Me again. Would you like some breakfast?"

"No, I have an early start at work and this conversation is making me late."

He squeezed past me, leaving the bathroom free for my morning routine. As I went back into the bedroom to collect my robe, I heard the front door slam shut.

Bye then.

As the week progressed things went from bad to worse. Conversation practically ground to a halt and a strange, unwelcome tension began to infect our once happy home. Even more worrying, Logan had started to spend most evenings away from the flat and I had no idea where he was. It's strange how something that would have seemed inconceivable just a week earlier had become a new normal. I accepted it because I had no choice. I couldn't understand what had caused this once warm, attentive man to become so cold and distant. He shut me out completely and there was no getting through to him. Whenever I tried to initiate any conversation, he would tell me not to question him. I learned that it was better for me to say nothing.

Logan bought a new mobile phone, and when it rang he would look at me, then at the caller ID and then leave the room to answer it. While my chats with him dwindled to nothing, he seemed to spend a lot of time on his new phone. After each call, he would immediately get ready and then head out once again. Then the cold calling started. One night, when he was out, the home phone rang, which was quite unusual. Hoping it might be one of my family, I answered it, but there was just silence at the other end. I put down the phone, thinking nothing of it. Then, half an hour later it rang again. Still no one at the other end. *That's strange, twice in an hour?* And that was just the beginning of the random silent calls that I came to dread.

I got into an empty bed yet again. I had stopped wondering where Logan was but I had never stopped hoping I would see the old Logan again, smiling at me and making me feel like the most special, the most loved woman in the world. How could we have moved so far apart in such a short time? I had never felt more alone or helpless. Was this how relationships worked? I had no idea. And, without my family to talk to, I had no one to advise me or make me feel better.

"Do you have a minute, Alice?" I knew my boss would provide the kindly ear I needed, so at work the next day, I resolved to confide in her.

"Of course, come and take a seat. What's up?"

"Well I'm not sure to be honest. Logan has been acting strangely recently and I'm not sure what's up."

"What do you mean by 'acting strangely'?"

"Just not speaking to me much, being moody, just not himself."

"Maybe he's struggling at work or something," said Alice. 'Have you tried talking to him?"

"Yes. He tells me to stop asking questions or ignores me."

"Hmm, yes that is odd. Maybe, like a lot of men, he finds it difficult to talk about his emotions."

"Well, he doesn't struggle when he's chatting on the phone to his friends and I presume he has plenty to talk about when he stays out all night."

Alice looked shocked. "How long has this been going on for?"

"A couple of weeks," I said miserably. "Alice, I don't know what to do."

"Okay, I think you need to sit him down and talk to him calmly. Maybe cook him his favourite meal to show him you care and have a conversation about what on earth is going on."

I felt lighter after talking to Alice, as though a heavyweight had been lifted off my chest. It had been good to share my worries and I also now had a plan, something I could actually do to try and get us back to where we were.

Knowing Logan's love of Italian food, I went to the supermarket after work and bought all the ingredients for one of his favourite dishes, chicken Florentine pasta, along with a garlic cheese ciabatta and a good bottle of red wine. I rushed home so that I had plenty of time to get everything ready for him. My heart was racing, my stomach churning. I hoped that this would do the trick and he would finally tell me what was bothering him.

What if he doesn't come home?

I pushed that thought out of my mind and focused on preparing the best meal I had ever cooked. With the food all prepared I turned my attention to the table, setting out a candelabra, the best cutlery and fresh, long-stemmed roses. Logan's favourite soft soul music was playing quietly in the background, setting the mood hopefully, or filling any awkward lulls in the conversation. With everything in place, I went upstairs to get myself ready. I needed to look my best; it would remind him of those early days when we would go out on dates and he always used to compliment me on how wonderful I looked. I knew the perfect outfit and rummaged around in the wardrobe until I found the classy but casual black dress that always made me feel good. I added pearl earrings and matching necklace, styled my hair into loose curls and made sure my make-up was perfect. I was ready – at least I looked the part, even if my wobbly insides didn't match.

When I heard Logan's key in the door, I called out to him that dinner would be ready shortly. Instead of going upstairs for his customary shower, he came and sat at the table, seemingly oblivious to all the trouble I'd taken to make it look nice. Taking a deep breath, I placed a plate of food before him and sat down opposite. I didn't take any food. My stomach was full of butterflies, not hunger – I would eat once we had talked. We sat in silence as he ate and tried to stay calm. Once his plate was empty and he had laid down his knife and fork, I began.

"Logan, I think we need to talk." "About what?" His eyes were guarded.

"About us, about our relationship. I just wondered if you were okay because you haven't been yourself recently."

Ignoring me, he picked up his plate and took it over the sink.

I persevered. "I just want to know if you're okay. Have I done something wrong?"

"DOES IT LOOK LIKE THERE'S SOMETHING WRONG WITH ME?" he roared, his nostrils flaring.

He was scaring me. *He's never raised his voice to me before.*

"No, it's just that you've been so distant recently," I said carefully.

"You're just a stupid individual, that's what you are!"

"No I'm not. Why are you saying this? What's the matter with you?"

"The matter? With me?" He suddenly threw his empty plate against the marble sink, sending shards of porcelain everywhere. "I'll teach you to question me!" he growled. Seizing both pots of food on the stove, he propelled them against the kitchen wall. I stood in speechless horror as I watched my carefully prepared dinner slide down the cream wall and onto the carpet. "Clean that up," he barked before striding off upstairs.

I fell to the ground, petrified by what I had just witnessed. I crawled towards the smashed pots and began to scrape the food back into them with my hands. The tears that had been gathering finally poured out when I cut my finger on a piece of broken porcelain.

Where has all this anger come from? He must be going mad. I've never seen this before in anyone. My father never treated my mother like this, nor my uncles their partners.

I managed to stand on shaking legs, wrapped my finger in kitchen paper and took out all the detergents in the cupboard. *I must clean all this up so he doesn't flare up again.*

After spending hours on my hands and knees, trying to make sure every trace had been cleaned away, I sat in the kitchen until darkness fell. Logan had stayed in, for once, and I tracked all of his movements around the house until I was certain he had gone to bed. Then I waited for him to fall asleep before creeping upstairs. I tiptoed around, getting ready for bed whilst trying desperately not to wake him. Slipping under the duvet, I kept myself as far away from him as possible. *Who is this man beside me now?*

What was I going to do? I had no one to turn to. I needed my mum like never before.

7

LEAVE A MESSAGE

Hello Mum, it's me, Amelia. Please don't hang up. I just need to talk to you. It makes me sadder than you can imagine that I no longer see or speak to you, or my siblings. I never wanted it, or meant for that to happen. I miss home, I miss you all and I think about you every day. I feel so alone, and you may say that this was my choice but you didn't leave me any choice. I didn't choose to leave you, I chose to be with the man I love. But he's changed and become someone I don't know any more. I'm frightened, Mum, and I don't know what to do. Please will you help me?

Too shaken by the night's events to sleep, I lay awake wondering how I could reach out to my mother. I really needed her support, but we hadn't exchanged a word since I had left home. I imagined all sorts of phone calls in which my mum would welcome me back into the family and help me to work out what to do. But after six sleepless hours, when the rays of sun began to peer through the curtain, my fantasies melted away. I couldn't simply wish everything better. This wasn't a fairy-tale. I had no special powers to deal with a man who smashed pots against a wall for no good reason. And I wasn't a little girl either. I had to somehow sort out this mess like a grown-up. I looked over and, seeing that Logan had already left for work, I breathed a sigh of relief. I knew there was no way I could go into work that day. I dialled Alice's number. *Please, please let this go to voicemail!*

No such luck. Alice answered with her well-drilled, corporate greeting. "Hello, this is Alice, how can I help?"

"Hi Alice, it's Amelia…" I tailed off, still unsure what excuse I was going to give.

"I was wondering when you were going to call. This is the first time you've not been here to open up with me. Running late are we? I hope it was a good night!"

I couldn't even pretend to engage with Alice's teasing. "I can't make it in today, sorry. I have to go now, I'll see you tomorrow." I ended the call before she could respond.

Downstairs in the kitchen, I was greeted by the food stain on the wall, mocking all my frenzied cleaning efforts the previous night. I had been too tired to tackle it the night before and today's morning sun revealed that the stain to be much worse than I thought. I suddenly felt a wave of utter hopelessness wash over me. *What's the point of me trying to make things better?* But I was scared of what Logan might do if he came home to find the evidence of his outburst still staining the pristine walls. In a panic, I rushed towards the cleaning cupboard, grabbed some products and scrubbed until the skin on my fingers was shrivelled from water and detergent. I was sitting on the floor, waiting for the wall to dry before scrubbing again, when the intercom buzzed. It was the postman, who had dialled the wrong flat for his parcel. Standing between the intercom and the phone on the hall table, I felt torn. I was cut adrift from my family, floating further out into the sea and though desperate to get back into their harbour, I wasn't sure it was possible.

Just call!

I picked up the receiver and dialled the familiar London number. In my heart I knew I had made the right decision, but my mind did not agree.

What are you doing? Remember what she said to you. There's no coming back from that.

I hung up. A moment later, as I walked back towards the kitchen, the phone rang. I didn't dream that it might be my mum – she didn't even have my new number. Thinking it might be Alice with a work-related question, I picked it up.

"Hello?"

"Hello, I received a call from this number."

Caller ID! "Hi Mum, it's me." "Amelia? Is that you?"

"Yes, Mum."

"The sun will always rise after winter. How are you?"

I had never understood that phrase growing up, but now I knew exactly what she meant: following the cold of an argument, things will always get sorted. It gave me hope to hear her say that.

"I'm fine, Mum, how is everyone?"

"We are all well, thank you. Why did you not wait for me to answer the phone? Did you not want to pay for the call?"

"No, Mum, not at all. I just thought you weren't home."

Letting that obvious white lie go, Florence said, "So how is Logan? Is he well?"

"He – yes he's fine."

"That didn't sound convincing. Has something happened to him?"

"He's changed a little bit."

"What do you mean by a little bit?"

"Well we used to go out a lot and we don't do that anymore."

"That's just the honeymoon period coming to an end," said Florence. "All relationships go through that."

"What I mean is, he still goes out, every night, but without me."

"Go on." The tone in my mother's voice had changed. "I hardly ever see him now. He comes in from work then goes straight out again and I'm usually in bed by the time he gets home. I've tried to get him to talk to me, but he won't. And then, yesterday…" I ground to a halt, afraid to hear my mother's 'I told you so'.

"What happened yesterday, Amelia?"

With a lump in my throat I told her, falteringly, about the disastrous meal and the pots being thrown. "He told me to clean it up and walked out," I finished.

"Amelia, are you at work?"

Did I mishear that? Why is Mum asking if I am at work? "No, Mum, I'm at home."

"So, you're telling me he threw the food you'd cooked, including your portion of dinner, against the wall." In my mother's eyes, wasting food was a sin and totally unacceptable. "Now," she continued, "you're telling me you're not at work. Why aren't you at work?"

"I didn't sleep all night, I was too scared. And I've spent all morning trying to clean the wall."

"Amelia, I don't like the sound of this. You sound like you're in danger."

Hearing my mum's voice again, so strong and steady, made me want to cry.

"You need to be careful," continued Florence. "You need to log in your mind everything that's happening and really make sure you're happy with the decisions you're making. I am here if you need to talk to me, but I cannot think for you."

I wasn't sure how she would respond to the favour I needed to ask her. "I know, Mum. But do you think you could speak to Logan about what happened?"

"Me? That's very risky, Logan and I have no relationship. What makes you think he will listen to me?"

"I don't know if he will. But I tried and look what happened. He respects his elders, so he won't be rude to you."

"Okay, call me when he comes home."

As I put the phone down, I felt glad that we had spoken and pleased that Mum had sounded happy to hear from me. *She must have forgiven me if she's agreed to talk to Logan.*

I distracted myself with housework until he arrived home and then timed the phone call perfectly so that it coincided with the moment he emerged downstairs after his shower. He came into the hallway, frowning when he saw me smiling and talking so freely. I made sure I peppered our small talk with 'Mum' so he knew who was at the other end of the phone. He had just marched past me towards the lounge when I said, "Logan? Yes, he's here, do you want to talk to him?"

Logan pivoted sharply to see me holding out the phone to him. He was angry that I had just agreed to him having a conversation without his permission. He gave me a devilish stare as he snatched the phone from me. It began safely enough, with Logan telling Mum about his new work project. I headed towards the lounge to avoid listening to the inevitable downturn in their chat. Suddenly Logan narrowed his eyes and said, "Yes, I did," and I knew Mum had dropped the bomb. I turned up the volume on the television.

Two ad breaks had passed before Logan put the phone down. I sat with my hands on my knees, my eyes fixed on the TV, bracing myself.

"Cry baby! Cry baby!" came Logan's taunts as he approached from the hallway. "What was telling your mother supposed to do? Did she tell you to run home? I didn't realise I was living with CCTV. Are you going to run crying to Mummy over every little thing?"

I didn't respond to his goading. After his flare-up the previous night, I feared that any remark from me now may tip him over the edge again. So as soon as he settled himself on the sofa I retired to bed. Not letting me get away that easily, Logan started to impersonate me on the phone to my mother, his mocking voice following me up the stairs.

The next day I went back to work, bringing good coffee from the delicatessen I passed on my way in. It was a peace offering for my boss and I hoped it would lighten the mood. Alice sat at her desk, her arms folded, and waited for my explanation. When I had finished telling her the unvarnished truth, she burst into tears.

"Amelia, I'm so sorry. It's all my fault. It would never have happened if you hadn't taken my advice."

Wiping away my own tears, I reassured Alice that it was most certainly not her fault. "No one could have predicted that. He's never behaved that way before, never even raised his voice to me."

It was a relief to tell the truth and clear the air. I hadn't felt good about missing work, especially without an explanation, and I didn't want it to threaten the trust between me and Alice. After a good long chat, we fixed our make-up and carried on with our working day.

A month went by and the tension at home remained. Every day played the same melody: we didn't speak in the morning and Logan was never home in the evening. Weekends were also spent apart. While Logan went out enjoying himself, I would do the housework, which had now become a source of fear for me because Logan had developed an obsession about everything being in its proper place. I was careful not to move or change any objects or furniture in the house, and if I slipped up I would be subjected to hours of shouting and swearing. Rather than phoning my mum with constant complaints, I endured my pain in silence. It was a lonely, lonely time.

I didn't think I could feel much more wretched, but then came a new low. I was startled from my sleep one night by a loud thump at the front door. The bedside clock told me it was 1am. Something wasn't quite right and Logan was not lying next to me. Was I going to have to deal with this by myself? Then I heard his voice from the hallway. *Perhaps he went downstairs to investigate.*

I was shocked to see Logan lying on the hall floor, his arms and legs flailing about loosely as he attempted to sit up. *Something's seriously wrong with him.* I rushed to his side and recoiled when the alcohol fumes hit my nostrils. He was twice my size and it took me a long time to manoeuvre his legs out of the doorway so that I could shut the front door.

Unable to understand his drunken mumblings, I rolled him onto his side, as I had been taught in first aid training. At that moment, Logan vomited his stomach contents all over the floor.

Holding my nose at the foul stench, I tried to clean up the mess with disinfectant, soap and towels. But some of it had already run underneath him, seeping into his shirt. Unable to move Logan, I cleaned his face and went to bed. It was hard to get the smell of vomit out of my nostrils.

I was woken at 7am by the sound of disgusting profanities. Logan barged open the bedroom door and it hit the wall with a smack.

"Why did you make me sleep on the floor, you waste of space?" he shouted.

I sprang out of bed, shaking. "I tried to move you but I wasn't strong enough."

"Liar! You wanted me to sleep down there, didn't you?"

Raising both of his hands towards my chest, Logan shoved me towards the bed and I hit the wooden frame with a sickening crack before sinking to the floor. "You good for nothing piece of rubbish," he sneered.

Shivering and sobbing, I curled up into a ball on the floor, an agonising pain scorching my back. *Is he going to kill me?*

As in a terrifying nightmare, I opened my mouth to scream but no sound came out. Slowly, painfully, I managed to crawl onto the bed and lay face down. Frozen. Logan left the room without saying another word.

I told Alice I had slipped getting out of the bath and she seemed to believe me.

"Still hurting?" she asked when she caught me wincing as I lowered myself into the new padded chair with back support that she had organised for me. "That must have been quite a fall. You need some of those suction handles on your bath."

"The doctor said I'll be fine, it's just bruising, nothing broken. Don't worry."

"But I have to worry about you," smiled Alice. "I have to worry about my top-performing girl. You sure you don't want some time off?"

"No, honestly, I've already had enough time off." "Amelia, that was one day!"

"One day too many for me. Besides, how would you cope without me?"

"All right," said Alice, knowing when she was beaten. "Just take it easy, okay?"

I hated lying to Alice when she was so good to me. I seemed to be telling untruths to everyone lately. I was even lying to my mum by not telling her what was going on. Keeping secrets, telling lies, this was not who I was. I thought about all the changes I had been making in order to cope with Logan's recent conduct. Now I had started compromising myself, my own integrity, and it was one compromise too many. I had been avoiding the problem, throwing myself into work and taking on any overtime offered to avoid going home. But now I couldn't look away any longer: it was time to do something about his toxic behaviour. The romantic approach had spiralled out of control, so I needed to do some straight talking.

I called him at work, knowing that would never act up in front of his work colleagues.

"Hello Logan, do you have a moment to speak?"

"Is there something wrong? If not, don't call this number. I am busy."

The line went dead. I was not going to be silenced, not this time. I told Alice I needed to leave work early to get some more painkillers. Another lie. I had never been to the doctor about my back. I was taking four paracetamol a day and pretended they were prescription tramadol. On the way home I bought a back support to try and ease my constant pain and took a taxi home to avoid having to stand on the tube.

When I arrived at the flat, I was met by a ringing phone but didn't answer it, aware that I had said I was going to the doctor. It rang out and then soon rang again.

"Hello." There was no reply. "Hello?" Still silence, so I hung up.

When it rang again, an unknown female voice said, "Is Logan there?"

"No he's not. Who's speaking please?"

Whoever she was, she hung up.

I soon stopped wondering who the caller was as I struggled to put on the back support, the pain momentarily pushing any other thoughts from my mind.

I had decided to wait for Logan in the living room and waylay him on the way to his evening shower. I was physically shaking at the thought of what was ahead, but I knew our relationship was worth fighting for. *He needs to understand that I love him but can't deal with the way he's been treating me recently. Not so long ago, we were inseparable and due to be married. I don't know what's happened to everything we had but I'm sure we can get things back to normal.*

I was full of nervous energy, unable to keep still. I rocked back and forth on the dining room chair, I paced up and down the living room, rehearsing speeches in my head. Until finally, the key in the lock. It was now or never. I met him in the hallway.

"Logan, may I speak with you?"

"About what?"

"Us."

"What about us?"

"Well, our relationship has changed a lot recently." Logan looked me dead in the eye and did not respond. Undeterred, I listed all the things I had rehearsed earlier.

"We don't go out anymore, we hardly see each other. You go out without me on a nightly basis and never take my calls. We hardly speak. You threw my dinner away when you were angry, you pushed me when you didn't believe I was telling the truth. You constantly swear and shout at me. I don't feel like you love me anymore and I just want things to go back to the way they were."

Logan stood as still as a statue, his eyes never leaving mine, his breath quickening.

"Also," I continued, "I wanted to ask you. When I have

been doing your laundry I have smelled an unfamiliar perfume on your shirts, and one of them had lipstick on the collar. Then we've been getting strange phone calls. When I pick up, no one answers. But today a woman answered and asked for you."

"Did she say anything else?"

"No, she hung up when I asked her name. Do you know who it was?"

"No."

"But you sound as though you were expecting her call."

Logan inhaled sharply. "Who are you talking to, Amelia?" "Pardon?"

"You heard me. Who do you think you are talking to?"

"I just wanted to know what's changed and if I need to do anything different to make it go back to how we were."

"Why were you answering the home phone anyway? Had you scheduled another cry-baby call with your mother?"

"No, I live here, so if the phone rings I'll answer it."

"Don't answer me back when I speak to you, woman!"

"I'm not answering you back, I'm answering your question."

The walls of the flat seemed to darken and close in on us. In the intense silence, I was aware of a dog barking outside, the drip of the kitchen tap and the gas running through the pipework. Any relief I had felt about getting everything off my chest, any hopes I had nurtured that we could forgive one another and move on, were all turned to dust when I looked at Logan. His face was reddened by the blood pumping through his veins, his breathing was fast and shallow, his teeth clenched.

By now I knew the danger signs, but I hadn't seen anything approaching this before. I noticed a drop of sweat trickle down his forehead as his right arm began to spasm. *Is he having a stroke?* I walked towards him so I could catch him if he fell. In that same moment, a gust of wind swept through the room and everything went black.

8

PARKING RESTRICTIONS

Blind… I can't see. Help me! Somebody help me! I've gone blind, I'm blind! I can't see! I can't feel my legs. I can't move. Why can't I move? What's wrong with me? Blood, I can taste blood. HELP! Why won't anyone help me? Am I dying? I can hear someone calling my name. Is that you, Daddy? Have you come for me? I can't see you. I can't breathe, my lungs don't seem to be working. I'm not ready for this, I don't want to die, not yet. Please, somebody help! I can hear sirens, voices. But it all seems so far away…

"Amelia, Amelia, can you hear me?" A voice was calling me from my sleep. I didn't want to wake up, I wanted to stay in that dark, warm, safe place.

"Amelia, open your eyes."

Please just let me stay here.

"Amelia, please darling." A different voice, one I

recognised. I fluttered my eyes open, but one of them seemed stuck together and would only open to a thin slit.

"Here she is. Hello, Amelia."

I'm looking at an unfamiliar face. A nice face, warm eyes, a smiling mouth. "I'm Mary and I'm a nurse. You've had an accident, Amelia, do you remember? And now you're in the hospital and we're going to look after you."

I opened my mouth to speak but my swollen lips seemed stuck together. An accident? No, I didn't remember. Was that why my whole body felt bruised and sore? Why did my eye hurt so much?

"Amelia?" said a concerned voice.

I slowly turned my eyes and saw him. Logan. His face was creased with worry, his eyes red. Had he been crying? "I'm sorry, I'm so sorry," he whispered.

Why was he sorry?

"I've called your mum."

The thought of seeing my mum brought tears to my eyes.

"Don't cry, darling, you're going to be okay," said Logan.

There was something hovering at the edge of my mind, gently nudging my memory. The phone, something to do with a phone call. An argument? No, I couldn't quite grasp it. As I sighed heavily Logan reached out to take my hand. His right hand. And then I remembered. That same hand that had slammed me against a wall until I sank to the ground. The same hand that had rained down blow upon blow upon me as I cowered on the floor, begging him to stop until, mercifully, I passed out. The large hand that now covered my small hand on top of the hospital blanket.

I tried to move it away from his grasp, but he held on

tight. I looked into his eyes and he must have seen the change in mine.

"I'm so sorry," he repeated.

I closed my eyes so that I didn't have to look at him. I had a hazy memory of a flashing light, someone in uniform, being in the ambulance and waking up to darkness, thinking I had gone blind. And in the background, Logan's voice, like a dark mantra, repeating, "She fell, she fell." I could still hear him saying it now, to the doctors and nurses, as I lay in bed. "It was an accident, she slipped and fell as she was getting out of the shower."

I was very tired. I didn't want to think about anything right then, I just wanted the pain to stop, I wanted to sleep.

"Amelia," said the soft voice of nurse Mary. "The police are here to see you. Are you able to talk to them?"

A male and female officer stood by my bed. "Sorry to trouble you, Miss Nazario, we won't be long. We just wanted to find out what happened to you, how you sustained your injuries."

"I've already told the officers who came to the flat, she fell in the bath as she was getting out of the overhead shower," said Logan. They clearly hadn't believed him.

"Her eye has been smashed to a pulp and she is covered in severe bruises," said the policewoman. "They seem excessive injuries for a fall in the bath."

"She fell badly and hit her eye on the tap," replied Logan.

No, I didn't! He beat me, he beat me unconscious.

"Strange that her hair was bone dry if she was coming out of the shower, isn't it, sir? You also said that the screams the neighbours heard coming from your flat was the television, is that correct?"

"That's correct."

"Miss Nazario, we would like your account of what happened tonight," said the male officer.

All eyes turned to me. "Could you tell us in your own words?"

What can I say? He's standing right there.

"I, I–" I stopped. My mouth was so dry, my voice barely a croak. "Please may I have some water?"

Someone handed me a plastic beaker and I drank it down gratefully.

"She's not up to this, can't you see that?" said Logan.

"This won't take long. Miss Nazario, how did you sustain these injuries?"

I was too afraid to say anything. I didn't want to lie but I certainly couldn't tell the truth. I was scared of what Logan might do and scared of what might happen to him. I could feel my breath quicken as the panic rose in my throat.

"I don't remember, I blacked out," I managed to say huskily.

The officers continued asking questions for a while, but when it was clear I wasn't going to confirm what they clearly suspected, they left.

There wasn't a part of my body that didn't hurt. I was exhausted and must have slept for a little while. I was woken by the sound of my mother's voice in the corridor.

"Where is she? Where is she?"

Florence flew into the ward, rushed over to my bedside and when she saw me she stopped dead in her tracks, as though all the air had been sucked out of her.

"Mum," was all I could say. I tried to stop the sobs that threatened to convulse through my body. She was here, my mum was here.

"Oh my girl," she said finally. "What happened to you?"

"She fell," said Logan who had never left my side.

Mum looked at him. "She didn't fall! I know she didn't fall!" She turned to me. "Did you?"

I couldn't hold back the tears any longer.

Florence sat down and said, "Tell me."

I wasn't going to lie to my mum, not again. "It was, it was… Logan."

"He did this? He beat you up?" I nodded, miserably.

My mum's eyes flashed. She shot to her feet and turned the full force of her fury on Logan. "What is wrong with you? Call yourself a man? What sort of man beats a defenceless woman unconscious? You're a disgrace. A poor, cowardly excuse for a man." She carried on with her blistering attack for a good few minutes, while Logan just stared at the floor.

When Mum was done, she sat with me, wetting my lips with water, smoothing my forehead, plumping my pillows. I loved her fussing over me, I felt like a child again. When she finally left, squeezing my hand and promising to visit the next day, Logan started telling me again how sorry he was. I didn't want to hear it, not then. The nurse came in and told him to go home so I could sleep, but he remained by my side.

The pain didn't subside. I was in agony from the beatings I'd taken all over my body. But it wasn't until I eventually looked in a mirror that the full horror of what he'd done finally hit me. When I saw my bashed-in face I became really angry. The doctors told me I was lucky not to have lost my eye. *My mother was right. What sort of man would do this?* Whilst furious with Logan, I was also angry at myself for being stupid enough to believe that I could mend our relationship with a good chat. *What a naïve fool I have been. How could I have got it all so wrong? I can never forgive him for this.*

But I was wrong. Logan stayed with me for the full two days I was in hospital. Two days of him weeping and saying sorry finally wore down my defences. I began to feel a bit sorry for him. His remorse seemed genuine. *He's really sorry and I do believe this has frightened him. He won't do it again. And maybe I provoked him, I didn't heed the warning signs when he told me to stop.*

As my physical pain diminished, my heart calmed. Even so, I wasn't quite prepared for the surprise Logan sprung on me just before I left the hospital. He was, as usual, sitting at my side. "Amelia, do you think you can ever forgive me?"

"I don't know, Logan, I think it will take some time."

"I want you to know that it will never, ever happen again. I love you, Amelia and I want to want to spend every day proving it to you." He took my hand and before I knew it, he had slipped something sparkling on my finger.

"Is that what I think it is?" I couldn't quite believe my eyes.

"Yes," smiled Logan. "Amelia, will you marry me?"

It was everything I'd ever wanted. I suppose we both knew what my answer would be…

I returned to the flat with mixed feelings, confused by everything that had happened. Despite my happiness at being engaged finally, I hadn't recovered physically or mentally from Logan's violence. Despite his recent flashes of anger, I had never seen that horror coming and it was going to be hard for me to completely forget about it. Something had been broken that night. *But perhaps my love is being tested. Real love survives through the bad times too, doesn't it? To love is to forgive and that's what I must do. I will keep faith in him and in our relationship.*

At first, I had been worried that our engagement was merely a show to keep me happy and that it would drag on for months with no wedding in sight. "If we are not married within a year I am going back home," I promised him. But I needn't have worried. Logan was keen that we should get married as quickly as possible. I would have liked more time to plan and look forward to it, but at least it was really happening. I told myself it would be a brand-new start. We posted the banns and sent out invitations to family and friends for a ceremony in four months' time. There was only one sticking point between us.

"No, I'm not getting married in a church."

"But Logan, it's what I've always dreamed of. You've already had your church wedding, don't rob me of mine."

"Exactly, I've done it once and that was enough."

I was disappointed, but I could see from the set of his jaw that he wasn't going to be moved. "Will you at least agree that I can wear a wedding dress?"

"You can wear what you like just so long as we marry in a register office."

My aunt Mabel and half-brother George came over from America for the wedding. Dad's older sister Mabel was the head of the family. A respected, wise figure, her word was law among us, so it was important to me that she approved of my match. Mabel couldn't understand why she hadn't met Logan and why the wedding was happening in such a rush. There was no way I could hide from her what he'd done.

"What?" she cried. "He hit you? And you're still marrying him? If I'd have known, this marriage would not be happening, that's for sure. But I guess it's too late now." "Please don't tell George," I begged her. "He's giving me away." My half-brother was also going to Logan's stag night.

"Are you kidding?" replied Mabel "I won't say a word. There's no telling what he'd do to Logan if he knew what he'd done to you."

The night before the wedding, when I should have been looking forward to the happiest day of my life, I was full of doubt and uncertainty. Could I be doing the right thing if the family elders – my mum and my aunt – were so disapproving? "Are you mad?" had been my mother's words when I had told her about the engagement. I didn't dare tell her the full truth, that two weeks after leaving the hospital, Logan had started abusing me mentally and physically all over again. This was a secret shared by just two people and neither of us were going to reveal it. As I lay in bed, I tried to quieten my busy mind and silence the doubts running through my head. *Am I mad? Why am I still going through with the wedding, knowing what I know? Because you love him, Amelia, despite everything you love him and that's the most important thing. And it will be different once you're married.* Resolving to try and simply enjoy the following day, I fell into an uneasy sleep.

The next morning, it didn't look as though the weather

was going to be on my side. "It's 11 o'clock on a very grey Saturday morning," said the cheerful voice on the radio. "There is a very good chance of heavy rain today, so whatever you are doing, make sure you take your umbrella." I looked at my reflection in the full-length bedroom mirror. My white dress was exquisite: the fitted lace bodice and long satin skirt fitted me like a glove, flattering my slender figure and accentuating my curves. The pretty headpiece I had made from tiny white flowers looked perfect on top of my long, glossy dark hair, which I'd styled in soft loose curls. My expertly applied make-up gave me a flawless radiance.

I looked beautiful, just as I had always hoped I would, just as I had always imagined myself looking from the moment I had first started dreaming of my wedding day. But I wasn't happy with the reflection staring back at me. *Still not enough.* I carefully applied some more foundation around my right eye. Today I needed all my make-up skills to hide the discolouration. At least the bruise was faded now. Two weeks earlier, it had been black and greyish blue, my eye swollen shut. I cast my mind back to the moment Logan had caused it. He had been talking on the phone to the mystery caller, the woman who kept phoning and leaving no message. When I asked him who he'd been chatting to, he became angry and told me to shut up. But I didn't.

"Was it her?" I asked. "Your secret caller?"

Logan poked his finger in my face yelling, "Shut your mouth or else!"

I couldn't help myself. "Or else what?"

He punched me, hard, in my right eye. The next thing I knew, the lights had gone out and I hit the floor. It wasn't the first time he'd hit me since I had come out of hospital, but it was by far the worst. Luckily, I'd taken a few days' holiday from the BBC to prepare for the wedding, so I didn't have to explain my horrific-looking injury. By the time I went back to work I was able to cover it up and carry on as if nothing had happened.

I would do the same today: cover up and carry on. What else was I going to do? The purr of an engine and the soft click of an expensive car door shutting told me that my limousine had arrived. There was a soft tap at the door. "Hi Amelia, the car's here, are you ready?" called George.

My stomach lurched. Was I ready? No, not really. On shaking legs, I left the house and got into the beautiful car waiting outside.

"You look stunning," said George.

There was such a strange mixture of emotions churning inside me. I was excited yet fearful, happy but also very sad. On this special day, I couldn't help thinking about my dad and felt his absence like a physical pain. I looked over at George, so smart in his suit, and I was so grateful that he had come all the way over from America to be here and to give me away. But it should have been my dad sitting by my side. *But face it, Amelia, if Dad were alive there would have been no wedding.*

The car pulled up outside the register office and suddenly I couldn't breathe. My heart was pounding against my ribcage. As George opened his door and prepared to step out, I said, "Wait." He stopped and turned to me, his face questioning. "I'm not ready to get out yet," I murmured.

George smiled at me. "It's okay to be nervous, Amelia."

Was this simply last-minute nerves? I called out to the driver, "Could you just drive about the block please?"

Without saying a word, George shut the door and the car pulled away from the kerb.

Trapped. I felt trapped. *I don't want to do this, but how can I not? Everyone's here and waiting, all the planning, the money spent. And where would I go? I can't go home again.* Once I realised there was no going back, I felt curiously calm. After all, I reminded myself once again, I was marrying the man I loved. It would all be fine, I would make it fine.

The car arrived back at the resister office and this time, I took the hand that George held out to me and emerged from the car. *You can do this. You want to do this. You love him.*

A sea of smiling faces greeted me inside the register office; all my friends and family were so pleased to be there and pleased for me. My mother's face was the notable exception: her face was stony as I slowly walked past her. And there was Logan looking drop-dead gorgeous. I was glad to see that he actually looked as nervous as me. We were in this together. Everything would be alright.

9

RESEMBLANCE

I can feel Mum's eyes boring into my back as I stand before
the smiling registrar. I know those eyes are asking the
question, "Are you really going to do this?" She doesn't
believe I should be marrying Logan. I hear her incredulous
words, "Are you mad?" *I don't know*, is the honest answer
to that. I can picture Aunt Mabel's worried face when I told
her about Logan beating me up. I can recall my dad's advice
about men: "If he loves you he will always treat you with
kindness and respect. Don't ever settle for anything less."
What am I doing? Please, dear God, let it be all right. I will
try my best–

Pardon?

I was suddenly startled out of my daydream by the sound
of the registrar's voice. "Amelia?" *Oh yes, that's right, I'm in
the middle of my wedding vows.*

"Pardon?" I said, realising that he must have been talking to me for a little while. Everyone, all our guests sitting behind us, laughed at my response. They must have been thinking that it was nerves, but although I was so scared that I could feel beads of sweat trickling down my back, I simply had not been listening to his words about marriage being a serious commitment. Instead I had been listening to the doubts in my head. The loud laughter helped to bring me back to earth and I gave the registrar my full attention.

A little later, he asked, "Is there anyone here with any lawful impediment to this marriage?" You could have heard a pin drop. I held my breath. The quiet seemed to go on forever. There was something wrong, there must be. I could feel it in the heavy silence. I convinced myself that everyone in the room was in on a secret.

They all know something.

A movement behind us broke the stillness and I turned to see the upright back of a lady walking quickly towards the exit and then disappearing through the heavy wooden door. I didn't know who she was, so she must have been one of Logan's friends.

I glanced at him and he didn't seem the slightest bit bothered about our absent guest, so I put it out of my mind. I was told later that it was his friend Edna, who had apparently been taken ill suddenly. The rest of the ceremony passed without further incident and seemed to be over in a flash.

"You may kiss the bride." Everyone clapped as we gave one another a shy kiss. Logan looked happy and I realised that, for the first time that day, I suddenly felt very happy, too. Happy and relieved.

The reception, in a hall in south London, was a joyous night. Everyone I loved was there, celebrating with us; there was plenty of food and drink and Logan was at his most charming. All doubts dispelled, I had a wonderful evening, laughing, chatting and dancing with my friends and family. That night, I had my first good night's sleep in ages and was looking forward to flying off to Tunisia the next day.

Logan had organised the honeymoon: two weeks in a luxury beach-side hotel. When we arrived there, the hotel was not quite as luxurious as the brochure had promised. If you looked closely, it was a bit tatty around the edges and the food was not exactly the highlight of our day. But we had a nice enough room with a balcony, so we could sit outside, smell the jasmine and admire the sea view. And in any case, we weren't going to spend long in the hotel, we wanted to get out and about. Well, that was the plan. And to start with, we immersed ourselves in all the new sights, tastes and experiences: a camel ride, a visit to a souk, checking out the local nightlife. I loved learning about new cultures, so I was in my element, starting to relax and have fun. We had a week of gorgeous honeymoon bliss, when Logan was his best, most affectionate self. I was so happy. Everything was going to be all right.

Then the itching started. "Logan, I really don't like this," I said, looking at the tiny rashes that were cropping up on my skin.

"Don't worry," he replied. "Just don't scratch them and they will go away."

But the rashes didn't go away; they spread over my body and became more fierce. Within a day or two my skin felt as though it was on fire and I was scratching it until it bled. "I think I need a doctor," I said when I could bear it no longer. "No," said Logan. "We're not calling a doctor." He was irritated with me, blaming me for spoiling his fun by allowing myself to become ill.

By this time I wasn't leaving the hotel. I was so sore and tormented and my skin looked awful. I didn't care what Logan said, I couldn't stand it any longer. I went down to the hotel reception and got them to send for a doctor. He diagnosed a heat rash. "Don't worry too much, just stay out of the sun." I didn't think it was a heat rash, but I had no other choice other than to stay inside and try not to itch.

Logan, meanwhile, didn't let my illness stop him from thoroughly enjoying himself. He completely abandoned me, going out on excursions during the day, then off out every night with the new friends he'd made. There was no support or sympathy, just annoyance that I was 'moping about with a long face' and other verbal abuse.

"Why are you itching so much?" he sneered one day. "You must be dirty."

Every night I sat in our hotel room, listening to the sound of people enjoying themselves down in the bar. Some honeymoon. I was utterly miserable, sore from my head to my toes, alone and sick in a strange place. I didn't feel safe and just wanted to go home.

The first thing I did on our return was to visit my GP, who told me I had caught scabies, probably from dirty hotel sheets.

"But why didn't Logan get it too?" I asked.

The doctor explained that some people get it and others

don't. "You were the unlucky one," he said. Shocked as I was, I now had a proper diagnosis and some comforting lotions to soothe my skin. I was also told to wash everything in the flat, to strip everything down, including curtains and make sure it was all cleaned. Slowly but surely I began to feel better. But it would be a long time before I could clean away the memory of my honeymoon from hell.

Once we were back into our normal routine, Logan returned to his familiar behaviour, barely speaking to me. He only paid me attention if he wanted to yell at me for, well, anything that didn't meet with his approval, from his dinner not being to his liking, to an ornament in the wrong place. I was trying to fight the feeling that I had made a terrible, terrible mistake in marrying him.

It was only a matter of weeks before I discovered I was pregnant. I was overjoyed and hoped Logan would feel the same way. Maybe this would change everything.

"Why did you get pregnant?" His face was thunderous.

I thought you would be pleased, Logan, like me. I was completely stunned by his attitude. I had just assumed that one of the main reasons for getting married was to start a family.

It was a lonely pregnancy. Logan carried on going out every night and the mystery calls increased. A woman's voice would ask for him and then hang up if he wasn't there, which he rarely was. Naïve as I was, the penny finally dropped that he was probably having an affair with this woman. I went to all the antenatal classes alone. I had asked Logan to go with me but he said, "No, it's not a man's thing." He didn't offer to drive me there either, even in the pouring rain, so I would go on the bus or sometimes walk when the bus didn't turn up. It was hard being in those classes, watching partners supporting one another and laughing together. Sometimes, on the way back, I couldn't help crying. I was now living so far away from my family that I had no support and, because I had always been working, I hadn't made any new friends in our neighbourhood. But I consoled myself that I was never completely alone – I had my precious baby growing inside me.

I was at home when my waters broke and I called Logan, assuming that this was enough of an emergency to bother him at work.

"Please can you come home, I'm in labour," I said. "Are you sure?"

"Yes, my waters have broken."

"And?" He had no idea what that meant because he hadn't been to any antenatal classes or taken any interest in what happens during birth.

"It means the baby's coming, so please just get here as soon as you can."

"Yes, all right," he said, reluctantly.

His baby is about to arrive and he resents being disturbed. What's the matter with him?

This was not the time to dwell on Logan's disappointing behaviour. My bag packed, I was ready to go, but terrified about what was to come. No childbirth classes can really prepare you for the enormity of giving birth for the first time. On the way to the hospital, I consoled myself with the thought that Logan would be with me all the way through as he'd promised. But once we'd arrived there and I was settled in a bed, he left, promising he'd be back in time to see the baby arrive. Another broken promise.

When the labour pains came I did not suffer in silence. I hollered and shouted and cried at the top of my lungs. The nurse was cross with me. "Stop your shouting," she scolded. "There are people trying to sleep in here."

But it wasn't as if I had a choice. I couldn't help but make a noise. The pain was just so overwhelming and the gas and air didn't seem to make much difference. I thought I was going to die with the agony of it. So I kept on crying out and the nurse kept coming in and telling me to keep quiet. Then, she suddenly slapped me, on my bottom, and said, "Shut up!" which made me cry all the more. I couldn't believe that she had actually hit me.

When my mum arrived the following morning, she could see how exhausted and frightened I was. "What's been going on?" she demanded. When I told her about the nurse slapping me, Mum hit the roof and told the nurse exactly what she thought of her behaviour. Then Florence took over. Holding on to me through the waves of pain, she calmed my panic and helped me to control my breathing. Hanging on to her every word and following her instructions, I had never felt closer to my mum, or more grateful for her. Unlike my husband, she stayed with me all the way through.

Logan arrived just as I was pushing our baby out. "It's a girl!" A healthy, beautiful baby daughter. It was the happiest moment of my life when she was placed in my arms. All the pain, everything, melted away. It was just me and my baby and pure love. I already knew what I wanted to call her. "Her name is Charlotte," I said. We all gazed at her. Yes, she looked like a Charlotte.

Logan held her for a while, his face soft. "She's beautiful," he said.

"He'd better start behaving himself now he's a father," said my mum after he'd left.

But the next day, when he came to pick us up from the hospital, Logan's anger once again showed its ugly face.

"It's not my baby!" he shouted, as he looked down at Charlotte. "It's not my baby!"

"What are you talking about? Of course she's yours," I replied.

"She's not, she doesn't look like me. I'm not her father."

I was at a loss. I had no idea what could have prompted this sudden outburst. And I couldn't believe what he was implying.

"Logan, what are you saying?"

At that moment my mother arrived and immediately sensed the tension between us.

"What?" she asked.

"Logan doesn't think Charlotte is his," I replied.

Instead of erupting, as I expected her to, my mother said calmly, "Why do you think that?"

Logan remained silent, though his body language told us he was wound up very taut.

"Is it her colour?" asked Florence, referring to Charlotte's very pale skin.

Again, Logan kept his gaze on the baby and said nothing.

"Listen," said Florence. "The children in our family are all born like this, with pale skin. Then the colour comes in and they get darker. So if it's the colour that's the problem–"

"It's not," snapped Logan. "She just doesn't look like me."

And that's when my mother erupted. She told Logan exactly what she thought of him and his 'insane accusation', and by the time she'd finished he had hung his head, all the fight knocked out of him. He never again suggested that Charlotte wasn't his. But the fact that it could even have crossed his mind meant that, for me, yet another light had gone out in our relationship.

I loved being a mum and I gave all of my attention to my daughter. Charlotte was my little princess, my delight, my joy, and I enjoyed every wonderful moment with her. While Logan continued to be distant and aggressive towards me, he took little interest in his baby girl. So it was up to me to make sure that my daughter received the sort of love I had been given by my own parents.

When it came to her christening, Logan wanted one of his friends as a godparent.

"Edna?" I asked. "Wasn't she the poor woman who was taken ill during the wedding and had to leave?"

"That's right, yes, but don't mention it when you see her, she's really embarrassed about it."

When I met her properly, before the christening, of course I didn't mention a word – I didn't want her to feel uncomfortable. I liked Edna, she was an old friend of Logan's from way back in Jamaica and they clearly knew one another very well. She was very nice to me and Charlotte whenever she came to the house to visit her goddaughter, and Charlotte really liked her. She was a good bit older than me and I came to see her as a sort of mother figure. I wouldn't find out until much, much later that Edna was anything but a mother figure...

Now we were a family of three, I knew we couldn't keep living in our one-bedroomed flat. Charlotte was sleeping in our bedroom and it would soon be time for her to have her own room. My suggestion that we move somewhere bigger was met with some resistance from Logan.

"We can't afford it, there's no money for that," he declared.

"I have money, my inheritance from Dad," I replied. "We could use that as a deposit."

Of course he quickly agreed to that, and we bought a nice, three-bedroomed house in south London, which I furnished with my own money. I loved our spacious new home, which gave Charlotte her own room and a lovely garden to play in. Logan wasn't so keen on my next suggestion, which was that I learn to drive.

"Why do you need to drive?" he said.

He feared that it would give me the very thing I knew I needed: my independence.

"Well, the buses are so unreliable around here and it's not fair to always ask you to take me everywhere," I replied. I didn't remind him that he was never here to take us anywhere. I had learned from bitter experience not to confront Logan. It was far better to keep the peace than to tell the whole truth.

The truth was that I lived in fear of Logan. And since my daughter had been born, my fear was much more intense. He never hurt Charlotte, but he created a harmful environment by his aggressive, cruel behaviour. On the rare occasions he was around, he never had a kind word for me, only criticism of what he saw as my failings. I learned not to answer back, or the verbal abuse just got worse. Thankfully, after Charlotte had been born, he had stopped hitting me. But that changed two years later. And once the violence started again, within sight of our young daughter, there was nothing left of my love for Logan. He had beaten it all out of me.

10

ROADSIDE ASSISTANCE

There's the front door. He's coming up the stairs, drunk again by the sound of his heavy, uneven tread. Holding on tighter to Charlotte in her single bed, I close my eyes and bury my face in her soft, clean hair, which smells of strawberry shampoo. *Don't wake up, princess, stay in your dreams.* I hear him stop outside Charlotte's bedroom door and I hold my breath. Pink fairy lights enable me to pick out the door handle in the semi-darkness. *Don't move, don't move.* After what seems like an eternity, I hear his footsteps retreat to the bedroom I no longer share with him. It's only once I can hear his loud snores across the landing that I breathe properly again.

They say that the apple never falls far from the tree. And if I wanted to understand Logan's violence and cruelty, I need look no further than his father Reginald. I remember, on our first date, Logan had told me that he wasn't very close to his dad. Logan may have had no relationship with his father, but he had inherited his worst character traits. When I first met Reginald, a few months into our relationship, I realised quickly that he was a vicious, angry and controlling man. Reginald didn't like me because he had really liked Logan's first wife and blamed me for breaking up his first marriage. However, in truth, their marriage was over long before I came into the picture. That didn't stop Reginald from abusing me verbally and taking any opportunity to belittle me. His wife, Deirdre, was a very meek woman who was obviously scared of her husband and would do anything to avoid his anger, including pretending to disapprove of me. They didn't come to the wedding; Deirdre told me later that she had wanted to but was forbidden by her husband, so they had sent Logan's aunt and uncle in their place. With such a role model as Reginald, it wasn't surprising that Logan turned out as he did.

I liked Deirdre. She was a nice lady, very kind, gently spoken and pretty. So I was pleased that she took a great interest in Charlotte and would phone me in secret to see how she and I were doing. Deirdre really wanted to see the baby, so one day we arranged for me to sneak round for a visit when Reginald was out. It was so moving to watch Deirdre's sheer joy at being with Charlotte, and she clearly adored her granddaughter. I only stayed for 10 minutes, scared that Reginald would arrive back and fly into a fury, just as Logan would have done if he had known that I was visiting his mum without him. So all of my trips were carefully timed to coincide with Reginald being out, while giving me enough time to get home before Logan arrived back from work.

One day, I plucked up the courage to speak to Deirdre about her son's behaviour. I told her how angry Logan would get over the smallest thing, how he would beat me up and belittle me and how frightened he made me.

"I'm shocked, but honestly not really surprised," said Deirdre when she had heard my story. "His father is exactly the same." She went on to tell me about Reginald's abusive, controlling behaviour, including locking her up and not allowing her out. "I daren't go against his wishes," she explained. "It's just not worth it because he punishes me so severely."

"I'm so sorry."

"I'm sorry for you too, Amelia. Logan is so like his father and I am begging you to please be careful, be very, very careful, especially now you have the little one."

On the way home, I thought about what his mum had said to me. *I'm already so careful around Logan. What more can I do? What's to stop me becoming just like poor Deirdre, a frightened little mouse?* My personality had already changed a lot since being with Logan. I was no longer the sunny, confident, easy-going person he had first met. I had become so quiet and withdrawn and was always slightly on edge. The change had not gone unnoticed by my sister, who could read me like a book.

"Is everything okay, Amelia?" asked Kimberly one day.

"Yes, fine, what do you mean?"

"Are you happy?"

"Yes, Kimberly, yes I am."

"Are you happy at home? Is he treating you well?"

"Yes, I'm absolutely fine."

Kimberly paused for a second. "But you're not fine, are you?"

"What do you mean?" I asked.

"You're not as happy as you used to be. You're sad, you never smile, you're just not yourself. Is he – is Logan doing anything to you?"

"No, of course not."

"Well then what are those marks that keep appearing on your face? You keep making excuses, but how many times can you walk into a door?"

I didn't really have an answer, so I just changed the subject. My sister would never press me to talk if I didn't want to, she would wait until I was ready. There was no way I could tell anyone what was happening, that Logan was beating me on a regular basis and treating me with utter disrespect. How could I tell anyone that? I felt too afraid and embarrassed. He was missing out on time with his daughter, too, and I couldn't understand that. Charlotte was such a source of joy; why would any father not want to share in that?

One day I took Charlotte to the park and watched a father playing with his baby, throwing him up into the air and catching him. The baby was loving it, chuckling with his whole body, which was making the dad laugh, too. Watching this happy scene brought tears to my eyes because I was sad for Charlotte: she wasn't adored by her dad in the same way. Much as I loved my time with my daughter, I was happy when the time came for me to return to work. It would be good to get out of the house, to be with other people and to focus my mind on something other than being a wife and mother. But it would be a wrench to leave my little girl. Since I was working shifts, I wasn't sure who could look after Charlotte and it had to be someone I could absolutely trust.

Logan decided it was going to be his aunt and since she was family, I knew her and she seemed nice, I agreed.

One afternoon, I arrived early to pick up Charlotte. My daughter was so happy to see me that she started to cry, which was upsetting enough. But then, right in front of my eyes, Logan's aunt walloped Charlotte a couple of times and said, "Shut up! Stop this rubbish, there's nothing wrong with you."

I couldn't believe my eyes. I was shaking with rage, while Charlotte was now sobbing as though her heart would break. "No, not my daughter, you don't touch my daughter." I lifted Charlotte into my arms and left without another word. She would never be returning there. Logan was cross with me for what he perceived as a snub to his family, but I was not going to be moved on this. He could do what he wanted to me, but I would fight like a lioness to protect my daughter.

Luckily, my sister Kimberly was able to look after Charlotte for me and I knew that, apart from my mum, there wasn't anyone I would trust more with my little girl.

My mother was also a good support to me. She had more of a notion of what was happening with Logan, though by no means all of it. She would sometimes speak to him about his behaviour, but it didn't seem to make any difference. 'Take care,' was her constant advice to me and I knew she prayed for me all the time. I do believe that Mum would have taken me back home had I asked, but I didn't. I was too proud. So she prayed and I put up with the hell that was my marriage.

If I had described some of Logan's vicious, controlling games, people may have found it hard to believe they were the actions of a sane man. For example, there was the time he meddled with my car. Despite his opposition to it, I did learn to drive and passed my test very easily. I loved driving and the freedom it gave me. I still had my own money, so I bought a small car and suddenly I didn't feel quite so trapped anymore. Needless to say, Logan was not pleased.

One day, the car broke down and I managed to pull into the side of the road. Charlotte was strapped into her seat in the back and the traffic was roaring past and I had no clue what to do. I got out of the car, but I didn't even know how to lift up the bonnet. I hated the thought of phoning Logan, but he had been a mechanic, so he would hopefully be able to fix it. Just as I was plucking up the courage to call him, a gentleman turned up out of the blue and asked if he could help. He clearly had some mechanical knowledge. He spent a long time looking at the engine, pulling the whole thing apart painstakingly until he discovered what was wrong with it.

"See this?" he said, holding up a tiny object. "This is what caused your car to break down. See how small this is? You would never have found it. It didn't just magically appear out of nowhere, someone must have put that in your engine deliberately. Got any enemies?"

"Is the car all right to drive now?" I asked him.

"Yes, you're all good to go. But if I were you, I would want to know who had done this."

I didn't bother telling him that I already knew. What would I say? Well actually, it's my husband and he did it because he wanted to – what? Spoil my day, take away my independence, mess with my head. Any or all of those answers could have been right. I had stopped trying to understand how or why Logan could be so cruel.

I didn't say any of that to this kind stranger who had saved me, I simply thanked him. "I don't know what I'd have done if you hadn't shown up."

"You look after yourself," he said. He stood and watched as we drove away. I realised I had never even asked his name.

When I finally drove home Logan was there, looking surprised to see me.

"How did you get here?" he said, frowning.

"What do you mean? I drove, of course."

"But how is the car working?" He had given himself away.

"You mean how is the car working when you had deliberately rigged it so that it wouldn't?"

"What?" he said, looking taken aback.

"I know what you did, Logan. Someone fixed the car for me and he showed me what you did. You put something in the engine that messed it up."

He didn't bother denying it.

"Why would you do such a thing?" I continued. "What if it hadn't just broken down? What if there had been an accident? You may not care about me, but Charlotte was in that car."

Caught out, he didn't even have the grace to look uncomfortable. He just laughed and said, "You were lucky, very lucky."

Lucky? I was married to a man who was so twisted that he rigged a car carrying his wife and daughter. Anything could have happened to that car. And for what?

"You could have killed us both."

"You're always such a drama queen," he said. "Your car broke down, get over it."

No, I really didn't think I was lucky. I preferred his indifference to his warped attention. I could handle him never being there, going out with his friends and coming home when I was asleep in bed. I had grown accustomed to that and it was safer than the alternative. Once he turned his attention to me, I knew it would mean trouble. So many times, I wondered what had happened to the Logan who had made me feel like the most special woman in the room, in the world. Now he made me feel like the most stupid, irritating, worthless person.

It didn't help that I had given up singing once I'd had Charlotte because the lifestyle wasn't compatible with being a mum. Logan had loved coming to my gigs. He loved the glamour, living the high life, hanging out with celebrities and influential people in iconic clubs and venues like Ronnie Scott's. He also loved it when people complimented me on my performance, basking in my reflected glory and even acting as though it was partly his, as though he had somehow had something to do with it. Once I stopped singing, I lost my sparkle for him and he lost his ticket to those golden circles that made him feel as though he was someone. For me, it had all been about the singing, the performing; for him it was all about being seen in the right place with the right people. Now that was gone, my value to him had diminished.

I never knew when he would lash out at me, though I feared it every day. I got used to treading on eggshells, trying to do nothing that would aggravate him. He didn't care that he hit me in front of my daughter and, even before she could understand what was going on, Charlotte was a victim herself because she was living in an atmosphere of hatred. I knew Logan had nothing to complain about around the house because my mum had trained me to be the perfect housewife. From a very young age, I made my bed and cleaned our home to her exacting standards. Thanks to Mum, I was also a very good cook. But despite all my best efforts to ensure things were just as he liked them, Logan would always find something to complain about. As far as he was concerned, a shirt collar that hadn't been ironed properly, a meal that wasn't quite as piping hot as he would like, were good enough reasons to punish me. If I was lucky he would just shout and holler, but on bad days I would end up bashed about and bruised.

Most of the time I just kept it all to myself and put on a brave face. "Yes, I'm fine," would be my smiling response if anyone noticed that I seemed a little shaky, or if I moved as though I was in pain. But there were some days when I just hit rock bottom and I wondered how I could carry on. It was on one such day that a friend of mine asked me if something was wrong. Instead of giving my stock response, I told her the truth. I hadn't intended to, the dam just broke and out poured all the horrors that I was enduring on a daily basis. When I had finished telling my friend everything, she didn't speak for a little while. Then she said simply, "Come to church."

I had finished with God when my dad had died. My father had been such a devout Christian, so committed to his church and, in my mind, it was a cruel God who had allowed him to die so young. So, while my mother took great solace from the church, I had turned my back on it – for good, I thought.

"I don't know if I want to go to church," I told my friend.

"Just come."

I was at rock bottom, I had nothing to lose by going back, so I took the lifeline that my friend held out to me. I was so glad I did. I remember my parents' church as being a stuffy, serious place, with a bit of tambourine bashing. Not this church. It was young, vibrant, full of joy and music. The first time I went there, I felt so uplifted. Here was a place of safety and light, a place of love and positivity, a community that would offer me an escape from the darkness of home.

I looked forward to my church services every week, and slowly but surely I began to feel better. I became more involved in the church, taking on positions of responsibility, until eventually I was asked to become a leader. After all the months of Logan's negativity, of him making me feel worthless, it felt so good to have people believe in me and to listen to me, to feel that I could actually make a difference. Gradually, I started to feel more hopeful, more confident and in control of my life. I even spoke up for myself sometimes when Logan launched an attack. He noticed the change in me and must have realised that it had happened since I had started attending church.

One Sunday, as I prepared to leave the house, he appeared at the door with Charlotte.

"What are you doing?" I asked.

"I'm coming with you," he replied.

"To church?"

"To church."

"But–" I didn't know what to say. He'd had no interest in the church before and I suddenly felt as though he was invading my safe place. I knew Logan though. The more I objected to something, the more he wanted to do it. It was like dealing with a self-obsessed teenager.

"But what?" he asked.

"Nothing. Let's go or we'll be late." I doubted he was going to church to pray for God's forgiveness. I couldn't stop him going to church with me and perhaps it would have a positive effect on him. It certainly couldn't do any harm. And it would take nothing less than a miracle to turn Logan into a decent human being.

To my surprise, Logan really immersed himself in the church. He got baptised and accepted the Lord and we both then started attending a mentoring group, when we would talk about our relationship and receive support. I was so pleased that the church seemed to be having a positive effect on Logan. He was still hitting me, but less than before. I was grateful for that.

11

NO U-TURN

The van in front of us has been stopped by soldiers and the people inside it are ordered out of the vehicle at gunpoint. They all look wide-eyed and terrified as they stumble out and stand in a line, as instructed. Then the soldiers take aim, there is a crack of bullets and the bodies crumple to the floor like rag dolls. Leaving the corpses where they are, the soldiers turn their attention to the next approaching van. Our van...

After seeing news reports of the Bosnian war, the atrocities committed – particularly against women and children – and the need to get aid to refugee camps, I decided I had to do something. I gathered together a group of people to drive over to Bosnia with vital supplies. The idea was to take as much as we could in a van, including medical supplies such as plasters and painkillers, non-perishable food and clothes. I asked everyone I knew – family, friends, everyone I worked with at the BBC – to donate clothes and I received hundreds of items. I took them all home, then washed and stacked them into nice neat piles so that they looked as good as new. Logan was one of the people who agreed to come with me. He hadn't suddenly developed a conscience, or empathy towards others – he was in it for the glory. He cared less about the humanitarian cause and more about people's good opinion of him. Like all bullies, Logan wasn't very confident underneath his swagger and he was really bothered about what everyone thought of him. So, in public at least, he always turned on the charm, and made a huge effort to appear thoughtful and caring. I knew how convincing he could be – hadn't he fooled me himself when we first met? When his family came over for dinner, I would sit and watch him playing the genial host, the loving husband, and it sickened me. But at least I couldn't come to any harm when there were other people around. Our church also thought he was wonderful and that we had a perfect, loving marriage. Only our mentoring group had any idea our marriage wasn't quite what it seemed on the outside. And he wanted it to stay that way.

"Make sure you keep your mouth shut on this trip," he said the night before we went to Bosnia.

"What do you mean?" I said, knowing perfectly well what he meant. While some people on the trip were from our mentoring group, there were other people coming who knew nothing about us. *Keep my mouth shut about you beating me black and blue. Keep my mouth shut that you don't have a civil word to say to me when no one is looking. Keep my mouth shut that you terrorise me.* I didn't say that, of course, it wasn't worth the pain that would follow.

"Just keep it shut or it's going to get worse for you," he snapped.

I would have preferred it if he weren't coming to Bosnia. I felt that, once again, he had muscled in on something that was important to me. But I also knew it would be good to have another man on the trip, someone else to share the driving and someone who knew about engines, too. In any case, I couldn't have stopped him.

My mother didn't want me to go. "It's too dangerous, Amelia. You have a little girl, don't be irresponsible."

"What about all those mothers in Bosnia, Mum? The ones who have been through hell and have nowhere to go? I have to do this."

Seeing my determination, she raised no more objections and agreed to have Charlotte while we were away. We prayed together the night before we went, which helped to calm my nerves. In truth, I was scared about going. I was worried that it wasn't fair to my daughter that both of her parents were taking the risk. To add to my doubts, I didn't have my pastor's support. He told me in no uncertain terms that it was a stupid venture and we were poking our noses into something that wasn't our business. But, despite all the doubts and disapproval, I still felt in my heart that it was the right thing to do.

It was a long drive to Bosnia in our hired van. The terrain was rough going and needed physical strength, so it was only the men who took turns to drive. It wasn't a pleasant journey. We slept in the van, went to the toilet in the bushes and washed ourselves with bottled water. At one point, when we were driving over the Swiss Alps, there was a heart-stopping moment when the van skidded on the ice and we were in danger of plunging to our deaths. But there was far, far worse to come.

We weren't too far away from our destination when we saw the van up ahead of us being pulled over by soldiers. It was clearly another aid van, though not from the UK. We had no idea that they weren't letting people past certain borders. We watched with unease as the passengers and driver were forced out of the van by armed soldiers. They were probably going to have to answer questions about the purpose of their visit. But we saw with mounting horror that they were being lined up against a wall. Surely this couldn't mean… Then came the rattle of the gunfire as they were shot dead, every single one.

There was a stunned silence in our van. We couldn't believe what we'd just seen.

"Turn back," said someone.

"And go where? They've seen us now."

It was true. As we drove towards the soldiers, they were waiting for us. A cold fear had wrapped itself around us. Were we next? My legs were like jelly when one of the soldiers gestured for us to get out, while his colleagues looked on, guns aimed. We could see the corpses lying on the ground as they marched us over to a different section of the wall and lined us up. Trying to keep my eyes averted from the massacred bodies, I looked at Logan and saw that all the colour had drained from his face. I thought of my little girl waiting for me at home. One of our group started to pray and everyone else joined in, apart from me. Charlotte was not going to grow up an orphan. I had to do something. One of the soldiers was saying something to us in his own language and I started to try and explain who we were.

"We're here to help," I ventured. "We have brought medicine, food, clothes." I pointed to my own clothes, trying to make him understand what I was saying, but it was no good. He carried on shouting at us and my increasingly emotional pleas were not heard. It all seemed hopeless. The whole thing was being observed by another soldier, a little distance away, who was clearly in charge. Then, suddenly, he snapped some sort of order and gestured with his hand that we should be let go.

I couldn't believe it. Our prayers had been answered. We didn't relax until we were in the van, driving away, and it was clear that the soldiers weren't going to come after us. Then our relief came gushing out, in tears and repeated offerings of 'Thank you, Lord'. Even Logan was crying as he accelerated away from the scene of terror. I felt guilty that my grand idea to come here had put everyone through such a terrible ordeal and, for the first time, I really questioned the wisdom of the trip.

But when we reached the refugee camp, all the doubts fell away. The women were so overjoyed to see us and they wanted to give us cups of sugar to thank us.

"No, no, there's no need," I said, knowing that sugar was priceless to them.

"You have to take it," said the camp leader. "That's the only way they can show their gratitude to you for what you've done." So we graciously accepted the small bags of sugar they pressed into our hands. We learned from the camp leader that, behind the smiles, many of the women were in a terrible state. A lot of them had been widowed during the war, some had been raped and had children from that abuse. Now they were all displaced, left with nothing and nowhere to go. We spent several hours in the camp. Though we didn't speak one another's language, we managed to communicate with the women non-verbally, through smiles and hugs, the squeeze of a hand, sometimes sharing tears. I was amazed by the women's courage and grace in the face of such suffering. It was a truly moving and humbling experience.

The journey back was drama-free and I was so pleased to arrive home. I hugged Charlotte very tight. Given all we'd gone through, everything we'd seen, I was just so thrilled and grateful to see my daughter. We had only been away for seven days, but it seemed like a lifetime. Despite all the difficulties, risks and heart-stopping moments, it had been the right thing to do. Our journey to Bosnia made the headlines. I was on the front page of newspapers, on the radio, even on a news special – the story was huge. I was overwhelmed by the media response and proud of what I'd achieved, but the main thing was that we'd tried to make a difference – and lived to tell the tale. I would never forget those brave women, the real stars of the story.

Although I was glad that I had gone to Bosnia, it stayed with me for a long time afterwards. Logan, meanwhile, just loved the fact that it made him look good. Throughout our journey he had posed as the model husband, calling me darling and sweetheart and being physically affectionate. When he kissed me or gave me a hug, telling me not to worry, I had no choice but to play along. To the outside, he was a wonderful fellow, which made my pain all the worse. Once we returned, he revelled in all the attention he had received and loved telling the tale in lurid detail. He was in his element playing the hero.

Logan wasn't the only one who enjoyed being in the spotlight after our Bosnian trip. Our pastor enjoyed going in front of the cameras and telling the reporters how proud he was of what we'd done. This was the same pastor who had told us not to go, that it was none of our business and that we were being stupid to even attempt such a journey. The same pastor who had refused to take my calls when I had phoned him during our trip, hoping that he would give us some strength and support. The hypocrisy was too much for me. I had a vain, deceitful man at home, I certainly didn't want another at my church. So I wrote the pastor a letter, resigning from my role as church leader. He didn't want to let me go, but the damage was done: he had lost my trust and respect.

Our trip to Bosnia did not bring Logan and me any closer. If anything, it highlighted the differences between us even more. The beatings carried on as before and one day, I decided I'd had enough. While Logan thought nothing of hitting me in front of Charlotte, I tried to ensure that she was always out of the way. When there was any danger in the air, I would send her up to her room. Even as he was beating me, I would be looking up to see where she was and if she peeked through the railings, I would try to reassure her, telling her, "It's okay, go back in your room." I tried to protect her as much as I could, but I knew her young eyes had already witnessed far too much. I could take the physical pain of

Logan's beatings, I had grown used to it; what I couldn't bear was to hear my daughter screaming and sobbing behind her bedroom door while it was going on.

This particular day, Logan was angry with me about something and as he approached me, I sent Charlotte upstairs to her room. As I tried to protect myself from his vicious punches, something in me just snapped. I rushed upstairs, grabbed Charlotte and ran out of the door. I ran all the way to the police station and was hysterical by the time I arrived there.

"I've been beaten up!" I screamed.

The police drove us back to the house with the sirens on. I got out of the car and stood at the door waiting for the two police officers. Logan must have heard the sirens and I didn't want to be first in, with him lying in wait for me. But the police were hanging back behind me.

"You go in first," they said.

"I don't want to, I'm frightened."

"You have to enter your home first, it's procedure. But we'll be right behind you."

So, holding Charlotte tightly, I stepped cautiously into the hallway. It was pitch black – the evil creature had switched off the electricity, all the better to terrify me. Walking into the darkness, knowing he was there somewhere, felt so eerie. It was like walking into a horror film. Both Charlotte and I started to cry.

"It's okay, just walk forward a bit," said one of the officers.

"I can't," I wailed. "If I walk forward he is going to kill me." I knew he was more than capable of it.

"We are right here with you, just walk forward so we can

come inside."

I stepped forward gingerly and they followed me. "We are the police, Mr Nightingale, please come out and show yourself." Nothing. Wherever he was, Logan was not going to show himself. Telling me to wait where I was, the police then started searching the house. I looked up the stairs and in the darkness I could just about make out a shape. *Is that him?* And then I heard something move.

"He's upstairs! He's upstairs!" I cried.

I clung to Charlotte as the police went up the stairs, trying to stop my trembling so that my little girl wouldn't feel any more frightened than she already was. The open loft hatch suddenly appeared in their torchlight and I saw an image that chilled my heart. Hanging down through the open loft was a rope tied into a noose. I couldn't contain my terror any longer.

"Oh my god, he was going to hang me!" I screamed.

The female officer tried to calm me down while the male officer called out, "Mr Nightingale, please come down." Still nothing.

"Mr Nightingale, if you don't come down we will come up there, and if we come up there, trust me, you're not going to like it."

After another small silence, Logan suddenly appeared at the hatch and lowered himself down. I took an involuntary step away from him as he looked over at me and his hateful expression sent a shiver down my spine. The police took him downstairs and asked him what was going on.

"Nothing," said Logan, with a smirk.

"What's that noose about?"

He gave a little laugh. "Nothing."

The police had heard enough. They arrested him and took him straight to a mental institution, where he was locked up.

It was strangely quiet in the house without him. I couldn't say it was peaceful because the memories of what had just happened seemed to hang in the air. But I felt relieved: at last I was free of him, free of the terror. I also felt uneasy and uncertain. They were waiting for me to sign the papers in order to commit him in the asylum fully. *I know he has done some terrible things, but is this the right thing to do?*

I phoned my mum and told her what had happened.

"You shouldn't have put him in that place," said Florence.

"I didn't put him there, the police did, because of what he'd done to me."

I spoke to my mum every day about what I should do. I was so conflicted. My mum thought that, as bad as Logan was, he didn't deserve to be locked away in a mental institution.

"Get him out, Amelia. He doesn't belong in there. He's young, he's got a good job, he's got his life ahead of him. If he stays there, they will fill him with drugs and he won't have any kind of a future. I mean it, get him out of there."

My mother was such a moral woman and so certain of what was right, that I did as she said. Instead of signing the papers to commit Logan, I brought him home. He was a very different man. Gone was the swagger, the shouting, the threats. Instead he was quiet and withdrawn, spending a lot of time on his own. At first he was quite weepy, and then he just seemed sad. He wasn't eating much either. After about a month I became quite worried about him. I called the doctor, who said he'd gone through a trauma and needed some time to heal. He took some time off work and gradually started to feel better.

Logan never did tell me what had happened to him inside the institution, but it had obviously shocked him, rocked him to his core. I can't say I was much happier living with the Logan who was a shadow of his old self, but at least Charlotte and I were safe. Then, as he started to return to the familiar Logan, the anger also returned and so, inevitably, did the violence. After eight months of relative peace, the hateful Logan emerged once again.

"I wish I had made you stay in that place," I said, the first time he hit me again. "You should never have come out."

Sadly, life with Logan was back to normal.

12

EMBEDDED WITHIN

I don't know myself anymore. Where have I gone to? What happened to the confident young woman who would stand up on stage and sing, who loved adventures and meeting people, who always pictured a bright, happy future for herself? Who is this timid person, afraid of speaking up for herself, afraid of hearing a key in the lock, afraid of the phone ringing…?

The beatings were getting worse. I never knew from day to day which Logan would be coming home. If I was lucky, it was the Logan who barely spoke to me or Charlotte, who would eat his dinner without a word, certainly not a thank you, and would then go out for the night. He wasn't even bothering now to hide the fact that he was seeing other women. The first woman, the mystery caller, hardly phoned at all now and she had been replaced by several others. If one of them called and asked for him, I occasionally challenged him about it.

"Who was that?"

"A friend."

"Are you seeing her?"

"Depends what you mean by seeing her."

"Are you having an affair with her?"

He would laugh. "So what if I am? What are you going to do about it?"

In the end I stopped asking him, because I hated to see his blatant lack of shame. I don't know why I hadn't seen it before, but Logan was a total womaniser: he knew how to play women and how to manipulate them. He could not only turn on the charm, he could read women well enough to know what they needed to hear. He had obviously got the measure of me very easily when we first met because I was an open book: naïve, trusting and inexperienced. It would never have occurred to me then that anyone would want to use that against me. I suppose I didn't see his true nature, not only because he hid it, but also because I wasn't looking for it. All too late, I saw him now for what he was, and he didn't even pay me the respect of hiding it.

On dark days, the Logan who returned home would be looking for a fight and I could sense it the moment he came in. The look in his eye, the set of his jaw, the tone of his voice. It wouldn't matter that I had rushed home early from work to make sure that his dinner was ready right on time, that I made sure it was the exact temperature he liked, that the house was as tidy as a show home. It wouldn't matter what I did: if he wanted a fight, then a fight he would have.

They were very one-sided fights. On those days, I knew that whatever I said would be wrong, so I said nothing and waited for the inevitable. I lost count of the amount of times he smashed his dinner against a wall or smashed his fist into my face. But as time went on he became more dangerous, more brutal. He just seemed to be so full of hate towards me. On one occasion he actually opened an upstairs window and tried to push me through it, breaking my tooth in the process. I fought back then and stopped him from ending my life, but how much longer would my strength hold out? In the meantime, I had joined another church and once again I found it a place of peace and joy, a safe haven away from the horrors of home. I felt I had a community again, and a valued place within it, and once again I became a church leader. Unfortunately, Logan also decided to follow me to church again and, just like the last time, he fooled everyone into thinking that he was a lovely person. But they weren't so impressed with him that they made him a church leader.

"They've made you a leader, why not me?" he complained to me in private. I decided it would be best to not even try and answer that question.

But this church also let me down when I needed it the most. After a particularly brutal beating from Logan, I decided to tell the minister exactly what was going on, hoping he would be able to talk some sense into Logan. But although he did call Logan and talk to him, the minister told me that I should follow the scripture, which says that a woman must be obedient to her husband.

"He's the head of the home, just as Christ is the head of the church," he said.

When I heard his words I felt so let down. *I poured my heart out to you, trusted you with secrets I haven't even told my own sisters and that's what you tell me?* I left his church immediately.

Feeling that the church had failed me again, I felt no desire to find another one. But I still had a need to connect with God in some way, so I started holding prayer meetings at my sister's house. It began with just a few people. I would sit with them individually and help them with their problems. Sometimes they told me what was happening, and I would listen to them and then offer up a prayer. Sometimes they wouldn't tell me they had a problem, but I would sense it and tell them what I felt was troubling them. That would usually end with the person crying and opening up to me. People told me that when I prayed for them, things changed for the better. I suppose I have always had an ability to sense what someone else is feeling. I guess you could call it empathy, intuition, compassion. But the people I prayed with called it something else.

Word got around that I had a 'divine gift' and then this small thing became so big, much bigger than I could ever have imagined. More and more people were turning up, all sorts of different people – religious and non-religious – all needing a prayer for one reason or another. People waited their turn outside the flat, and the queue went all the way down the stairs, out into the street and snaked down the road. It was amazing. What was so beautiful was that it was so simple, just me and one other person sitting in my mum's empty bedroom (we had to move her furniture out beforehand).

I loved helping people feel better and it's something that I truly believe I was born to do. Before things became really bad with Logan, I had worked with the homeless charity Centrepoint and had volunteered for the Salvation Army, going out into the streets at night to support those in need. It was just a natural thing for me to do, I didn't have to think twice about it. I do believe I was born for a purpose, and that purpose is to help others. When I sit with someone and pray for them, I feel a light within me that's very hard to describe. It's love, it's a warm ray that sends out healing. I take great joy from sharing this grace and am thankful for whatever it is inside me that enables me to do so.

Much as I loved praying for people, these sessions took a lot out of me because I was giving all my energy, my heart, to each and every person. At the same time, I was a working mum and my own time was in very short supply. I had been made redundant from the BBC and had taken on another hospitality position, this time in a hospital in West London. It was another demanding job and yet I was spending more and more time in prayer. Eventually I got to the point where I realised I couldn't carry on as I was, I would have to make a choice: I could keep my job at the hospital or perform my pastoral care full time.

But how could I leave my paid job to do something that didn't earn me a penny? I needed to support my family. I never received any money for my prayers. To me, asking for money would have been completely against the spirit of what I was doing. Then, a strange thing happened. People started leaving me donations. They felt so blessed that they wanted to show their gratitude by leaving me gifts of money. And

I was receiving quite enough money to take care of myself and my family. So I left my job at the hospital and devoted myself entirely to helping people. I was truly living by my faith because I was living entirely off donations, and I never knew if I was going to get anything at all. It didn't matter. I wasn't doing it for the money. I was doing what I felt I was destined to do, and I was very happy. I knew that, somehow, I would receive what I needed.

It was indeed a leap of faith to quit my job, because it wasn't long after leaving that I discovered I would soon have another little mouth to feed. Sometimes, out of the blue, the violence would stop and Logan would suddenly become more like his old self, warm, charming and loving. During those times, I allowed myself to hope that we might have finally turned a corner and I soaked up his affection like a sponge. As a result, I became pregnant again and I couldn't have been more thrilled, despite who the father was. Charlotte had brought such joy into my life and I couldn't wait to hold a baby again, even though it was Logan's. I expected him to fly into a rage when I told him, but he was surprisingly calm about it, almost pleased.

"Hopefully, this time it will be a boy," he said.

I didn't mind either way, but I hoped, for the baby's sake, that it was a boy.

Our wish was granted. I was delivered of a beautiful baby boy and we called him Mateo. Once again, I was filled with such amazement and an overwhelming love for this tiny little bundle in my arms. *I will protect you and your sister, Mateo.*

Then my life took another surprising turn. I had moved out of my mum's bedroom and hired a hall for my prayer meetings. We prayed and sang there; it was a joyful place and filled with a wide variety of people. I noticed that there was a man who started coming. He was short and bald with very pale skin. Although he was powerfully built, he seemed gentle and he had a nice way with him. He would just sit very quietly, watching what was going on. One day, after prayers, he came up to me.

"Hello, my name is Reverend Tom," he said. As I shook his hand, I couldn't help noticing the colourful tattoos all over the back of it. "I wonder if you'd like to come to my church," he continued. "I would like to invite you." I hadn't been expecting that, but I found myself immediately liking this softly spoken, charismatic man.

So I went to his church, which was in Mitcham, South London, not too far away from me. He was there with his wife, who gave me a smiling welcome, and he took the service, which I enjoyed very much. Rev Tom asked me if I would come again the following week, which I did, and then I kept going back every week. I was still doing my own prayer meetings, but there was something that drew me to Rev Tom's church.

Then, one Sunday, he said, "Amelia, will you take the service for me?"

It felt like a huge step to me, one I wasn't ready for. "I can't," I said.

"Yes you can, I know you can," he said.

And maybe, somewhere inside me, I knew I could, too. I was so nervous beforehand that my palms were moist and my legs were shaking. But as soon as I started talking, focusing on what I was saying and the people I was saying it to, all the nerves just melted away. It all just seemed to flow out of me and before I knew it, the service was over. I felt elated afterwards.

"That was wonderful, Amelia," said Rev Tom. Then he said something very surprising. "What do you think about maybe training to become a minister?"

Again my first reaction was to take a step back. "I can't."

"I really think you can. Look what you did out there today, you were wonderful."

"I did enjoy it."

"You have a natural gift and all the makings of a minister. Leave it with me, I'll look into it."

He discovered that I would have to undergo practical training with him, as well as study and sit some exams.

"It's completely within you, Amelia, you're halfway there already."

"Would I be able to continue my prayer groups?" I asked him.

"Of course. Look, I know you would be a fantastic minister, Amelia, but it has to feel right for you. Just think about it, discuss it with your family and let me know what you decide. But I really hope it's a yes."

There was a lot to think about. Me? A minister? In my heart it felt right and made complete sense. But it was a big commitment when my life was already pretty full. And the long training was quite a scary prospect. But then, I had never been afraid of a challenge or hard work. I went home and told my family (but I didn't tell Logan) all about it and they all encouraged me. With their blessing, I gave Rev Tom the answer he had been hoping for.

Rev Tom turned out to be an inspiration, and I couldn't have had a better teacher. Having previously been in the Navy – hence the tattoos on his hands and all the way up his arms – he had a life experience that really helped him in his work as a minister. Over two years, I had the privilege of being trained by Rev Tom and watching him at work in his church. He was such an inspirational speaker because he didn't separate himself from his congregation, speaking rather as one human being to another. "I'm still learning too, Amelia," he used to say to me. He always had time for everyone, but he also taught me how to manage my time, because being a minster brings many other responsibilities besides praying with your congregation. But perhaps the most important lesson I learned from watching Rev Tom was that key to being a good modern minister are the qualities of kindness, compassion and non-judgmental listening. "You have those qualities already, Amelia," said Rev Tom. "You can't really teach them."

The academic side of the training was hard, but I already knew a lot of the scripture-based content because of going to my parents' church when I was younger. We went through the entire bible from beginning to end. I spent many long nights studying in the run-up to the exams and to my complete delight I passed them. I also had to bring a sermon before a board of 12 ministers who assessed my delivery, historical context, understanding, research and the ability to relate it to the present-day audience before me. That was a very nerve-wracking day. But exams and assessment passed, the council approved me as a minister. The day I was ordained as a pastor was such a wonderful moment for both me and my family.

My mum and sister Kimberly came to the ceremony, along with Alice and my children. I took an oath to be minister of the gospel, was anointed and presented with my collar and certificate. When I looked over at my mum, I thought she was going to burst with pride.

I became a paid, full-time minister working for the church, but outside of church I also continued my separate prayers with the people who wanted to see me individually. If that meant praying with someone at 2am, then that was what I did. It was sometimes hard juggling everything – my job, my prayers, making sure I also made time for my children, as well cook dinner for Logan – but I managed it somehow.

Then, as if that weren't enough, I decided to start my own church. I do believe that everything that had happened in my life had led me to that point. It was important to me that the church was non-denominational, that it was free and that the doors were open to all. I wanted everyone who came to feel loved and to know that there was hope even through the darkest times. I also wanted to encourage people to be who they were. The Sunday service would be nothing like the dry, boring experience I remembered from my parents' church. Instead, it would be an uplifting experience, full of life and colour and music, with lots of young worshippers, too. And it wasn't going to be held in a traditional church. I found a school hall that was perfect – it even had a stage and lights. Our first service there was packed, and the church continues to this day, still going strong, with all the colour and positive energy that I had hoped for. Music plays a big part in what we do and there's often a lot of young people with tattoos jumping about! If an act of worship sometimes resembles a rock concert, that's fantastic – it's still an act of worship. I try to base my sermons around today's issues, so everyone, whatever their age, can relate to them. And they are not too long – I don't want to bore people. I try to make them positive and inspirational, full of joy and humour.

Throughout all of this, my mum was behind me every step of the way. While Logan never stepped foot in my church, nor showed the slightest interest in my ministry, Mum encouraged me in everything I did and always pushed me to do my best. She even became a pastor herself eventually. She would stand really close with me in the church and that gave me such reassurance, especially on the couple of occasions when I was about to do a sermon and doubted myself. Florence was having none of it, and would say firmly, "You can do it, just go up there and open your mouth." My mum's faith in me helped me to believe in myself. I finally felt as though I was on the right path, the path I was always supposed to be on. My belief in myself suddenly awoke. Despite what Logan said, perhaps I wasn't so useless after all.

13

TOMORROW MORNING

I know it's wrong to hate, but I can't help it, I hate him. I detest him with all my heart and soul. I hate him for using me as a punchbag, but even worse for allowing our children to see it and be afraid. I hate him for speaking to me as though I am a piece of dirt. I hate him for making me scared to be in my own home and for robbing me of my confidence. And most of all, I hate him for taking away my hopeful light, that good part of me that always saw the best in people and thought that love and kindness could turn any situation around. I pray that tomorrow, when I wake up, he doesn't. I cannot stand the sight of him any longer.

May God forgive me, but I hope he dies.

Logan started hitting me again just nine months after the birth of our son. It came as a shock because he hadn't hit me all the way through the pregnancy, and he had been so overjoyed to have a son that I thought, hoped, something in him had shifted. How wrong I was. If anything, the abuse worsened, and now Charlotte was of an age when she could really understand what was happening.

Although he never actually hit the children, they must have been affected by his behaviour. Charlotte was a very quiet, reserved child, who spent a lot of time reading, writing and drawing, while Mateo grew up with a fear of the police because of the number of times they had arrived at our house following a neighbour's complaint about the screaming. As a little boy, Mateo would cry whenever he saw police cars or officers.

But if Logan wasn't changed by Mateo's birth, I was. A mother's love is stronger than a man's fist. I would protect my children at all costs. And I would protect myself. Not long after Mateo was born, Logan proved to me that he wasn't really capable of caring for any of us. I woke up one morning and didn't know what had happened. My face was numb, twisted and a bit droopy. I couldn't eat or drink without making a terrible mess. One of my eyes was half shut and I was unable to speak properly. I was so scared and pleaded with Logan to take me to the hospital, but he told me not to be so stupid.

This went on for a few days, with me feeling wretched and frightened, but despite my pleas he would not take me to the hospital. I didn't have the strength to argue with him, so I called Kimberly and told her what had happened. It was quite hard to talk because of my droopy face, but I managed to make myself understood.

"What?" said Kimberly is disbelief. "What is the matter

with that man? Let me speak to him."

By the time my sister had finished with Logan, he was ready to take me to hospital, where I was diagnosed with Bell's Palsy. I was given steroids and it took three long months before there was any sign of recovery. During that time, my mum would come to check on me because she was so worried. She didn't quite understand what Bell's Palsy was and she thought I'd had a stroke. But that wasn't the only thing troubling her.

"Amelia, you can't stay in a marriage when you are suffering like this," she said one day. "You need to get out." Hearing this from my mum, who didn't really believe in divorce, was very powerful.

I knew, deep down, that something had to change. Even though Logan had done his best to make me feel stupid and worthless, I still had some self-worth within me. And enough was enough. I was worth more than this misery. As the months went by, this little nugget of strength and resolve grew bigger as I determined that we would somehow leave this toxic situation. I just had to come up with a plan.

Abuse thrives on silence, so the first step was to ask for help. I decided to confide in Alice. My former boss had become a friend as well as a colleague, and I was delighted when she had started coming to my prayer meetings and then my church. I knew that she had some inkling that things at home were not right. After telling her about that first violent incident with Logan, when he threw the food against the wall, I had never told her how much worse it had become. But she must have noticed my bruises, despite my best efforts to cover them up. Every now and then, she would gently ask me if everything was okay, and when I tried to reassure her that I was fine, she would just say, "You know, you can talk to me about anything if you ever need to."

Now was that time. I went for a coffee with Alice and told her everything. She cried at some points in my story and when I got to the end she said, "Amelia, you poor thing. I'm so sorry."

"It's okay, Alice, I'm going to leave him, I've decided. I'm getting me and the children away from him. But I need your help."

"Anything at all, just say the word."

"I have to plan this very carefully. Logan may be unhinged but he is a very cunning man. I need to do this properly because I want to make a clean break and I will only get one chance at this. So, I need to be smarter than him."

I had always earned my own money and though most of my wages went on running the house and bills, I had managed to squirrel some of it away over the years, knowing that I might need some escape money one day. So I began renting a flat in north-west London, a good two- and-a-half-hour drive away, for us to move into eventually.

I also told my sister exactly what had been going on. She, too, had known that all was not well at home. She would often help me cover my bruises before I gave a sermon in church, asking no questions, knowing that one day I would tell her.

"I never imagined it was as bad as this," said Kimberly. "Oh Amelia, I can't believe you had to go through this all on your own. I don't know how you could have stood it for so long."

"I was ashamed and afraid to tell you," I said.

"Ashamed?" said Kimberly. "What have you done that you need to be ashamed?"

It is very hard to explain to someone that continued abuse grinds down your self-esteem and makes you feel so worthless that, on some level, you feel that you deserve it.

"I'm going to leave him," I said. "I have a plan."

"Just tell me what you need me to do."

It felt so good to have finally broken my 10-year silence and, now that I had some support and a plan in place, our escape somehow seemed much more possible. Alice was a wonderful listening ear throughout this time, and she reminded me that our mutual friend, Justin, drove a rentals van, so he could move my stuff when the time came. I had got to know Justin through Alice and when I called him to ask if he could move me, I told him briefly about my situation. He was appalled and only too happy to help. "And if you need to get out of there in a hurry, just call me," he said.

One afternoon, I arrived home from work with the children and couldn't get into the house. Logan must have sensed that something was in the air because he had changed the lock. I had two hungry, tired children with me and no way of getting in. I was furious. *He's lost his mind. Locking us out of our own home? The home he wouldn't have without my money? He's really crossed a line this time.*

The time had come. I drove all the way back to Kimberly's house in north-west London and let her know that we would be moving out the next day. I called Justin to check that he could bring the van, and I also spoke to Alice, who had promised to help us on the day. Finally, I called a locksmith to help me get into the house in the morning.

I didn't sleep a wink that night. The van was going to arrive as soon as Logan had left for work and then we had a few hours to pack everything and leave before he came back. So I knew the whole thing was very high risk: there was a lot to do and very little time to do it. It relied on Logan going to work at the usual time. If he went any later, or not at all, then we had no chance.

The next day, we drove carefully into our road and I was relieved to see that Logan's car wasn't there. All systems go. I had arranged for the locksmith to meet us at the house, but before he would get me in, I had to prove to him that I lived there. "There's an alarm just inside the door," I said. "If you let me in I will turn it off with the code, and then you'll know I live here."

Justin turned up with the van, as did Alice, and once we got inside, we all set to work. When I saw them all there in the hallway, ready to give me all the help I needed, I could have wept. I was so grateful to Kimberly, Alice and Justin. But there was no time for emotion. Aware of how high the stakes were, we were all quiet and focused as we went through the house, piling things into bags, cases, the boxes I had been collecting. We all had our ears open, listening out for a car pulling up outside, a key in the lock telling us that the worst had happened and Logan was back. Luckily, all was quiet. So far, so good. We kept going.

"Let us know which bits of furniture you want us to take," said Justin.

"That's easy. All of it." "All of it?"

"I paid for every stick of it."

The sofa got stuck in the front door and, try as we might, we couldn't seem to get it through. The clock was ticking, we didn't have time to waste on one piece of furniture.

"Let's leave it, it's just a sofa," I said.

"No way, he's not getting it," said Justin. Through sheer determination, he managed to wiggle and inch it through the doorway. His grin was so huge and triumphant that it made me burst out laughing. I felt quite hysterical, but managed to keep my bubbling emotions under control until every last thing was in the van. I gave everyone a huge hug. We'd done it!

But just as we started the car engine to drive away, we hit a problem. Mateo started sobbing very loudly and let us know that we had left one essential thing behind – his potty. He had been inseparable from the thing all day, carrying it around from room to room, but somehow, in the rush to get everything done, it had been forgotten. Though we were terrified that Logan would suddenly appear, we had no choice – we had to go back in and rescue that potty. I would have laughed if I hadn't been so frightened.

Once the precious potty was safely in the car with us, we finally drove away. But there was just one more thing I had to do. I asked Kimberly to stop the car at the police station before we set off northwards.

"I have just left my husband," I said to the officer on the front desk. "And I am here to confirm that I have taken all the furniture because it's mine, I paid for it all. So if my husband tries to tell you that it's been stolen, he's lying."

I was so familiar with Logan's devious ways, I was pretty sure that he would try and report all the furniture stolen so that he could claim off the insurance.

I was right. We had only just arrived at the new flat when I received a call from Logan on my mobile. I braced myself to take it. *Let's get it over with.*

After calling me an unspeakable name he said, "You think you're so clever, don't you, telling the police there was no break-in."

So I had been right. Logan was nothing if not predictable. "It was mine to take, Logan."

He seemed to care more about losing the furniture than the children.

"I'll get you for this," he hissed. "You will live to regret what you've just done."

"I've had many regrets since I met you, Logan, but leaving is one thing I know I will never regret."

Before he could start swearing at me again, I ended the call.

I was so tired, but I also felt elated, as though a rock had been lifted off my back. After all the planning, the worry, the nerves, the risk, I could finally relax. I looked at my children as they explored the bright, modern flat that was to be their new home. Mateo was carrying his treasured potty from room to room, following Charlotte around. He had been an angel all day, not a single cry, not one grizzle from him (apart from the Forgotten Potty Disaster). And Charlotte had been so grown up, even though she was confused about what was going on. I was so proud of them and so relieved that I would never again go to bed wondering if this was the night their father would harm them – or leave them without a mother. We were away, we were safe and we were together.

The unpacking could wait. I knew what we all needed now – a snuggle on the sofa with some fun telly. "Who wants pizza?"

14

TITLE CHANGE

I wake up with a jolt. A noise has disturbed me – what is it? A scream, one of the children. Is there someone in the house? Is it him, coming home drunk? I must get to the kids… It's only when I have thrown back the duvet and placed both feet on the bedroom floor that I wake up fully. *No, wait. Relax, Amelia, just breathe.* I listen – no, there's nothing. I hear the unearthly scream again – it's just a fox. And I remember. We have escaped. We are safe. I lie back, my heart thumping. The fox is quiet now, nothing breaks the perfect peace. I fall back into a deep sleep.

Once we had left Logan, I started to enjoy really long, deep sleeps for the first time in years. However, I did wake up in a panic every now and then, switching immediately into that familiar frightened mode. I loved our new home and felt very secure there. But I had spent so many weeks, months, even years, in such a state of fear and unease that it took a while for it to work its way out of my system. When I was with Logan, I'd felt afraid more often than not, but I thought at the time that I was handling it all right. It was only now I had my freedom that I realised I had been living in a state of tension every hour of every day. I had just buried it deep down inside me. Even when I was at work, I would be worried about what might be waiting for me when I returned. And once I'd had my children, the fear was much, much worse. I had been living under Logan's tyranny ever since I had moved in with him.

It was such a beautiful, wonderful relief to be away from him, to know that I would never, ever have to live in fear of him again. That he was out of our lives and couldn't touch us.

When I told my mum that we had left Logan, she said, "I'm glad, Amelia, I thank God that my prayers were answered."

Hearing the relief in her voice made me realise that she had been scared, too. I felt glad that I hadn't told her the half of what I had been living through for the previous 10 years.

We settled quickly into our new home and life carried on pretty much as before – I went to work at the church and the children went to school – but now there was one important difference. I was no longer pretending that everything was normal and fine – everything really was normal and fine. I was so blessed to have my sister Kimberly because she took care of Charlotte and Mateo while I went to work. It was a long day for all of us. Many's the time there were tired tears in the car – not always the children's! But it was all worth it to keep my family together. And hopefully, there would soon be some money to contribute towards our upkeep.

I knew that Logan would fight tooth and nail to get as much as he could in our divorce settlement. I was prepared for a fight. I would have walked away with nothing if it had just been me, I was just happy to be free of him. But I needed to provide a home for our children and I needed to support them. I knew I couldn't rely on him for anything, nor did I want to. Unfortunately, Logan had enough money for a fancy barrister and I could only afford an ordinary solicitor, so I knew that the odds were already stacked against me. But crucially, I also knew I had right on my side. After everything he'd done to me, he surely couldn't win. There was no way.

Then, on the first day of the final hearing, came a terrible blow. My solicitor was sick and wouldn't be coming to court. I couldn't believe it. Any hopes I had for a fair settlement vanished. They were trying to find a replacement solicitor for me, but it was such short notice that it seemed like an impossible task. I was standing in the corridor of the courthouse, trying to fight back the tears. *What on earth am I going to do?*

Then, who should come striding over to me but Logan, the last person I needed to see. He had a nasty smile on his face, so had obviously heard the news.

"I hear your cheap solicitor hasn't bothered to turn up," he sneered. "So my barrister says it's now a done deal – you will lose and I will get everything. I said you'd be sorry you'd left me. Now is when you pay."

As soon as Logan had walked away, the tears started flowing down my face. I felt embarrassed to be crying in a public place, but I really couldn't help it. I had pinned all my hopes on this court hearing, that the law would make sure we were provided for, after everything that had happened.

"Are you all right?" came a man's voice. He wore a smart suit, bespoke I was guessing, and had an air of quiet authority that made me trust him immediately.

"No, not really," I sniffed.

"Can I help? My name is Richard Sullivan, I'm a barrister."

"Amelia Nazario."

"You look as though you need a friend, Amelia, or at the very least a cup of tea. What do you say?"

I nodded gratefully.

"Come on then."

He led me down the corridor and into an office, where he made us both a mug of tea from a kettle in the corner.

"Right then, Amelia. Start from the beginning."

So I did. I told him everything and he listened intently. If I skipped over something, not wanting to take up too much of his time, he would ask me questions that filled in all the details. He didn't express any opinions as I spoke, he just nodded and encouraged me to keep going right until the end.

"I'm so sorry for everything you've gone through," he said. "I want to help you. It just so happens that I am unexpectedly free at the moment, so I'll represent you."

"You will?" I couldn't believe my ears. But I didn't see how I could accept his kind offer – I didn't have the money for a barrister.

He obviously knew what I was thinking. "And I'll do it for nothing," he said.

"Mr Sullivan, I don't know how to thank you," I said, on

the verge of tears again.

"Well you can start by not crying again, I do hate to see a woman cry." He smiled. "From what you've told me, we have every chance of winning this. Now I need to get hold of all your case notes."

One little stroke of luck can make a huge difference if it happens at the right time. I was so lucky to meet Richard Sullivan, so lucky that he was a good, honourable man who was driven by his sense of justice to help me – for free. As it turned out, he was also a very good barrister who was more than a match for the opposing counsel.

The court proceedings were very painful for me. It was so hard to hear the harrowing details of my abuse, so hard to hear Logan's fictional side of events. Although he didn't actually want custody of the children, it was in his financial interests for him to try and get it in order to avoid paying the high maintenance the court would award if I got custody. To do that he had to portray me as a bad mother.

"She works long hours and always leaves them with her sister; she never spends any time with them," he said when questioned by his own barrister. "When they arrive home, they are so tired and it's just not good for them."

Then it was my barrister's turn to ask the questions. "Mr Nightingale, do you work, too?"

"Yes."

"So how would you expect to look after them if you had custody?"

"Well, I would work less and my family would help out."

"Is this the same family that struck Charlotte and reduced her to tears on a regular basis?"

Logan looked uncomfortable. "That was blown out of all proportion–"

"When you and Ms Nazario shared a marital home, how many times did you put the children to bed, Mr Nightingale?"

"I don't remember. I worked late."

"Oh, you worked late, and in your case that is acceptable, is it? Isn't it the truth, Mr Nightingale, that you have played no part in your children's daily care, that Ms Nazario was always responsible for all of it, even though she worked, just as you did?"

By the time Mr Sullivan had finished with him, Logan was sweating, the charming Mr Nice Guy smile wiped off his face. He also tried to portray me as a depressive, an idea that my barrister picked apart.

"Was Ms Nazario ever diagnosed with depression, Mr Nightingale?"

"I don't know, but she was always crying for no reason and it scared the children."

"Do you think the children may have been scared because they witnessed you beating their mother black and blue, Mr Nightingale? Indeed, may I suggest that your regular physical violence towards her, along with your bullying and intimidation, may have been the reason for Ms Nazario's so-called depression?"

"She made all that up, she's twisted things to make me look like the bad guy."

"I have police reports detailing regular visits to your house after complaints from neighbours about screaming and fighting. I also have witness statements describing the bruises that would appear regularly on your wife's face.

Are you really denying that you ever hit your wife, Mr Nightingale?"

He denied everything, but his words sounded hollow. Even so, just hearing his lies made me shake with anger. His barrister also tried to show me in a bad light, but I stuck to my truth. When all the evidence had been given, the judge went away to consider her ruling. It was a tense wait.

"I think you have a really good chance of winning," said Mr Sullivan. "But I should warn you that it's very rare for anyone to walk away with everything."

"I don't want everything, I just want what's fair," I said. "And I want them to know I'm telling the truth."

When we came back into the court to hear the ruling, Logan was doing his best to look confident and unconcerned. But his fake smile soon faded. The judge did believe me and awarded me everything – all the assets, including the house because of all that I'd been through.

"Obviously, it is very unlikely that Ms Nazario will want to return to that house, so you will remortgage it and give her all the money so she can rebuild her life," said the judge. "And you will pay all her legal costs." He was also ordered to pay maintenance for the children until they were 18.

I looked over at Logan and saw that the blood had drained from his face and he was in a state of total shock. His barrister was saying something in his ear as he looked over at me, his eyes full of hate. I gave him the faintest smile and turned away with my head held high.

I had won! It wasn't just about the money, or having some financial security, although of course that was important. But it was also about justice being served and people knowing who Logan really was. After all those years of suffering in silence, his abuse had been acknowledged and that felt fantastic.

With the divorce finally over, we did indeed get on with our lives. Using the money from the settlement, I bought a house in Dertham. It was a lovely, three-bedroomed semi in a quiet cul-de-sac with a nice garden that we all enjoyed. I found a nice school for Charlotte and Mateo and, with Kimberly's help, we all settled into a peaceful life.

The children were happy in their schools and at home, and I was enjoying my ministry in the church and my pastoral work. As a single parent, it could get a little lonely at times, but I didn't dwell on that. I still felt so lucky to have escaped the hell of my marriage, I was in no hurry to get tangled up in someone else's life again. A little bit of loneliness was a small price to pay for my independence.

My life was so fulfilling that I didn't waste any time thinking about the past, or Logan. But then a year after our divorce was finalised, he came into my life again. I heard through a mutual friend that he had prostate cancer and wasn't very well at all. This news stirred up a confusing mixture of emotions. There was a time when I might have wished harm on Logan, but those times had long gone; I had moved on. I was hoping one day to forgive him for what he had done, but in the meantime, I had let go of all the anger and pain. I wasn't sure if I wanted all those emotions stirred up again, but at the same time I also felt that I should contact him if he was ill. Then my heart just kept saying, *No, protect yourself, he's not worth the pain that this may cause.* And so my thoughts whirled around in confusion as I wrestled with my conscience. *What would Mum do?* I knew exactly what Florence would do – the right thing. She would put her own fears second and help another human being who was suffering. And whatever else he was, Logan was still the father of my children.

I was very nervous when I called him. *What if hearing his voice triggers something in me? All that pain that I buried deep within me.* There was only one way to find out. I took a very deep breath and dialled.

"Hello?" It was him.

"Hello Logan."

"Amelia, is that you?"

He recognised my voice straight away. "Yes, it's me. I heard you weren't well."

It was strange to hear him, sounding exactly like himself, but maybe a little more fragile. And as we talked about his health, I was relieved to realise that this man who used to dominate me now had no power over me at all. I was no longer under his spell, or stuck in his toxic games. I could see him clearly now for what he was – a weak, cowardly man who would never get under my skin again.

We caught up on news, chatting about various people we knew.

"How is Edna?" I asked. I hadn't seen or heard from Charlotte's godmother since I had left Logan.

"I don't know, I don't see her anymore."

"Why? You were such great friends." I remembered how he used to go and stay with her for weeks at a time in Jamaica.

"No, we weren't friends. I was having an affair with her."

"What?"

And so then the whole truth came out. She was the mystery caller, the woman who kept asking for Logan and hanging up. He had been having an affair with her for many years, even before we got together.

"But she was married," I said, "you were always talking about her husband."

"No, she was never married. I wanted you to think she was so you wouldn't suspect. But she wanted to marry me, in fact she told me not to marry you. She also said it was a mistake having a baby with you."

"So you mean all the time she was coming to our house, cuddling Charlotte, being so nice to me, she really wanted to break up our family and be with you?" I was incredulous.

"Yes, but when you left and I didn't want to marry her, we had a huge row and broke up," said Logan.

"And you asked your girlfriend – or should I say, your lover – to be our daughter's godmother. How could you?" This was a new low, even for Logan.

So there it was, at long last, the truth. It stung even more to think that I had actually liked Edna, when all the while she had wanted me out of the way. It was a shock to hear it, but then again, when it came to Logan, nothing should have surprised me.

Sometime after our call, I heard through the grapevine that Logan had recovered. Two years on, I called him to arrange for him to see Charlotte and Mateo. We met in a McDonald's near Oxford Street. Charlotte was very quiet around her dad, while Mateo was his usual lively self. The atmosphere was a bit stiff and awkward at first, but things were starting to get a little warmer when I suddenly noticed that Logan was wearing a wedding ring.

"You're married," I said.

"Yes."

"Since when?"

"A year or so."

Wow, you didn't waste any time, did you? "Who is the lucky lady?"

"You don't know her."

I looked at the children, who were listening to every word.

"So did you have a big celebration?" I asked.

"No just a small one, family only."

I looked at him. "And yet your children weren't invited. In fact, they weren't even told about it."

He had the grace to blush. "It was just a small thing and anyway, I didn't think they'd want to come."

He was the same old Logan – keeping secrets, telling lies and not doing the decent thing. As we drove home, I counted my lucky stars that I was free of this man and would never again have to worry what he was up to.

Released from Logan's bullying was like being freed from captivity, and I finally began to feel like my old self. It was as though I was thawing after a long freeze. I laughed more and was able to truly relax and be happy. I also had a real need to try and make up for lost time. Logan had stripped me of my self-esteem and I was going to get it back, one small step at a time.

One of these steps was to continue learning. I loved keeping my mind active and learning new things whenever I had the chance. When Charlotte was very young I had attended evening classes in reflexology and herbalism, which I had enjoyed hugely. I suppose I was interested in subjects that helped other people. I had always felt a responsibility to look after others, perhaps because I was the oldest child, a role that took on more weight once Dad had died. But my younger brother and sisters might say it's just because I am bossy! Once we were settled in Dertham, I took a course in counselling, studied hard and passed my diploma. In between my work at the church, I also did some voluntary work with the homeless. Then, after several rewarding years as a pastor, I was given the honour of being ordained a bishop. I was to be consecrated at a special church ceremony to which family and friends were invited. I was the only person being consecrated that day, so the service felt very personal to me.

It was such a special day. During the ceremony, 10 bishops laid hands on me and prayed, which was the most extraordinary feeling. Then I was presented with my bishop ring, my purple robe and cross and ministerial stall. It was a very proud moment and I was glad to be sharing it with my family and friends, who were sitting in the congregation. There was my mum, so wise and such a strong support, my sister Kimberly, whose unfailing love and generosity had helped me through the worst possible times, and my dear, dear friend Alice, always there with kindness and help when I needed her. And there were my children, Charlotte and Mateo, lights of my life, my greatest joy of all. I felt so proud and happy, full of gratitude and love.

15

THE FINAL CURTAIN

As I reminisce on my past, I hope my experience will be an inspiration and comfort to anyone who is suffering or has suffered any sort of abuse. I know from experience that when you are in the grip of an abusive relationship, you feel helpless to change anything. When someone treats you as if you are nothing, you begin to feel like nothing. You can free yourself from the misery, but you can't do it without help. I suffered in silence for more than a decade and it was the most lonely, terrible experience. If I hadn't had my children, I don't know how much more I would have suffered. But I left it until there was a do or die situation and then I made my choice.

I refuse to be defined by those years when I was a victim. There were times when I couldn't see any hope at all, when life was so dark that it was hard to put one foot in front of the other. As far as I could see there was no way out.

It has been hard work and has taken a lot of inner strength, but I am now living the life I was destined to live. I am incredibly blessed to have had a brilliant family and friends to help put me back on my path.

Abuse can happen to anyone, and if you are the victim of it, there is nothing in the world to be ashamed of. To anyone in an abusive relationship I would say, please don't suffer in silence. There is support out there. The most important step is the first one – asking for help. It takes courage and faith to take that first step, but I am the living proof that it is worth it.

Now here I am, happy, fulfilled, independent and at peace. I have been able to make a difference to many people's lives with my ministry. I have two wonderful children, who are amazing human beings and are fulfilling their potential.

That chapter of my life is closed, but my story doesn't end there...

Printed in Great Britain
by Amazon